Hood Girls Do It Better

A Hood Girl's Guide to Success

EPIPHANY KENDELL

Contents

Preface

Success: The achievement of something desired, planned, or attempted

Success is what you make it, baby girl. When you get straight As and Bs in school, you are successful. When you overcome heartbreak, depression, and low self-esteem, you are successful. When you go from sleeping around with different guys due to a lack of self-love to becoming celibate and waiting for the right one, you have succeeded. Do not allow anyone to define what success is in your world.

When I learned that I did not know everything, when I learned to accept my faults, when I learned that it isn't all about me and how important it is to give back, and when I learned to listen is when I became successful. One of the results of me becoming successful in those areas is this book and all of the amazing connections I have made that helped make this possible.

Hood Girls Do It Better

This is not only the title of my book or a slogan for promotion, but it's a movement that helps lift those of us from the hood up, reminding us that just because we come from what people say is the bottom doesn't mean we have to conform to the ways of it. Those of us who come from the struggle and fight our way through it succeed very well at whatever we put our mind to, because we know we don't want to go back to what we came from. So many ask, what is the it that I speak of? Anything that you want to put your mind to.

Acknowledgments

I want to thank everyone who has helped me make this possible—from being there to listen to my thoughts and ideas, inspiring me, listening to my troubles, and helping me link with other people to help me make this possible.

Ma, Daddy, Big Pootah, Sis, Woat, TT, Sean, Uncle Sha, Anthony, Chaka, Nee Nee, Raven, Mikuel, Aunt Tracie, Jasmine, MP...

Introduction

Hey sis, it's me, Piff. I'm watching you grow and mature. Your breasts are coming in, butt poking out, and hips and thighs swelling. You went from hair bows and braids to wash 'n' sets and weaves. The guys on the block are watching you; your curfew is later. Now you're into house parties and sippin' coolas. The flyboy with all the girls caught your eye. Yes, I know, and no, you don't have to hide it. I'm here for you to put you on to what life after you jump off the porch is like and what it's hittin for.

And for you, sis, who jumped off the porch into a pile of nothingness or trouble, I am here to help get you up out of that, because as you grow and mature you will realize that we females need one another more than you think we do.

I wrote this for you. I wrote this to let you know what it's really like out here, to let you know that you aren't the only one feeling the way you feel. There are females with far deeper stories than mine, but I'm stepping up because if I don't, who else will? People are going to be saying, "I knew it," or "Yeah, she was always fronting." But just like any other time, I'm going to laugh, because, at the end of the day, I am going to make a difference as well as have a better chance at succeeding at everything I do in life. The same ones sitting back and judging are the same ones with skeletons busting out of their closets, the same ones who aren't going far in life. So! Thank you to those of you who are reading to get a better understanding of me.

In and Out of Love

Guys

"Guys will always be there; focus on you." —Epiphany Kendell

Now, isn't this is a subject we females—young, old, black, white—love to talk about, whether it's a bad situation or a good one? I became friends with a lot of females from starting conversations about guys. The key to dealing with guys, no matter what age you are, is to focus on *yourself* and the things you have going on in school and after school. If you don't have anything going on, *go get into something positive!* Guys are usually a distraction to us females from a young age. A guy will go through difficult situations, but he will get and keep his life in order without a problem; he will stay focused and get things done. No matter what! A new girlfriend won't stop him and neither will a bad breakup. But *us!* Oh lawd, the whole world feels like it's crashing down when we go through a breakup.

We can't eat or sleep, we don't want to go out (or that's all we want to do to numb the pain); we just aren't ourselves. And when it's new with a guy, all we do is daydream and want to text or call him. We write his name with ours on paper and start thinking of the future and how our babies will look. Guys are the total opposite, sis. They think about sex and what's right now. I am here to tell you from experience that as long as your mind is focused and as long as you are busy with school and following your dreams, new relationships, heartbreaks, and breakups won't be as hard, because you'll be too busy to sit around and think about it. Everytime my ex and I broke up, I was fine because I had school, work, and partying, and I was dating. Any time I got involved with a new guy, I'd be so busy he'd be the one always reaching out to me. Guys will always be there, and the more you have going for yourself, the better the quality of guys you will more than likely come across. I have dated different kinds of guys: the flyy guys, the bad guys, older guys (because I was always mature for my age), the good guys, the successful guys.

In my experience, the flyy guys just want to get flyy. They'll spend their last bit of money on the latest fashions. These kinds of guys get on my nerves because they look like money but don't have any. They don't have a savings, they don't have investments, and they usually are young and dumb. The only thing they have to show for whatever money they had is their wardrobe. The bad guys are just what they are—hard on the outside, scared to open up, usually into things they aren't supposed to be into. The successful guys are a whole other story. I've dated guys with a 401k and their own businesses, and each of them thought, in their own way, that because they had money and I was young and not settled, they could say and do whatever they wanted. So I had to show them that yes, I am young; no, I am not settled and do not have as much money; *but* I am far from stupid and I am not naive. I've had guys putting money on the table to "invest in my business" and in the same breath throwing it out there that they want to have sex with me. They had me twisted. Even at a young age, I knew that selling your soul for something you can work for isn't the way to go. That's why I was able to stay on top of game, and that's why men have always respected me. Older guys like me because I'm a go-getter and ambitious, but at the same time, just like the successful guys, they think they can get one over me because they've been here longer than me. *Not!*

I remember there was this one guy I was talking to on the low. He so-called "wanted to hang out," so we went to a hotel, which I wouldn't have done had he not lived around my way and knew my family. I brought my business plan because he said he was interested in investing. Guys will try and use things you love or things you are interested in as bait to get in between your legs and in your mind. It's all about control. So we were in the hotel chilling and catching up, and I could tell he wasn't as interested in my business as he had pretended to be. When it was time to go to sleep, he thought he was getting some. I kindly shut him down and we left the next morning. Going with him, even though I did tell my friend who I was with and where I was, was dangerous. It didn't matter that our families knew one another. Anything could've happened. Until this day, he and any other guy I've dated or dealt with, respects me and my grind because they know what it is. They know I have respect for myself, so they have no choice but to respect me and what I am about.

Guy Friends

When it comes to guy friends, it can be tricky, because it will be easier to fall for him. He knows everything about you and you know everything about him. When either one of you is let down by someone you're dating, you have each other to go to. Dating a best friend, meaning a guy you never looked at in an "I like him" way, can be a great thing. If things don't go right though, you can lose a friendship, so tread lightly. I have *always* had more guy friends than female friends. Oh gosh, I remember so many people speculating, "I know she's fucking him" or "I know she's a hoe, hanging with them." That's why I do not judge certain situations, because I know how it is to be judged.

Guys with Girlfriends

A few of my associates have been in situations when a guy they wanted to date had a wife or a girlfriend. It *always* either ended badly or drifted off. How long can you play the side chick? I know there are women who really play wifey number two for years and years because it's convenient. The guy comes and spends a few days, pays a few bills, leaves shopping money, and then goes back home. I *always* press any female in that situation to not take it further. Out of respect for yourself and the other female in the situation, you should always stand up and say *no* to a guy who is trying to cheat on his lady.

My point to you, sis, is to find out ahead of time if a guy has someone exclusive like a wife, wifey, girlfriend, main chick, whatever! And if he does, dead it right there. If you meet a guy and he lies to you about not having a girlfriend, even though I know it might be hard, walk away. I am telling you, it is not worth it. Cut him off! I've seen situations where the main chick goes crazy and tries to kill the side girl. Even if the main chick is you, sis, you don't know where your mind will take you when your heart and feelings get played with. I always said I wouldn't go crazy over a guy, but when I was put in a situation where I found a pair of jeans left by a girl at my then boyfriend's house, I had to talk myself out of going upside his head. I said *"Wow,* this is how women black out," and now I do not judge women who do crazy things when a guy pushes them to the limit, because I see how easy it is. That's why it's really good to stay in prayer and to ask for guidance at all times.

Dating

"Dating is all about the chase, it's fun!" —Lauren Conrad

So a guy is interested in you and wants to take you out to enjoy your company. Either he lets you pick the spot, or he surprises you. You two have fun, and he takes you home to *your* house. That's it! Not to his crib or his man's or friend's crib, or anyone else's that isn't yours. It doesn't matter how much he spent on you; you do not owe him anything but a "thank you" for a great night. I've dated a few assholes who thought that because I let them take me out, they deserved some of my goods. That's when I had to get real boss and put them in their place. I didn't care what his title was or whether he had a lot of money or not. I don't allow anyone, especially a man, to think I owe him anything—especially sex because of a date.

If he wants to pay for sex, he should get a prostitute. Do not fall victim, sis. Another thing I want to address is that when you're dating a guy, date him for about one year before you get serious. Become friends, because you want to be able to see who he really is and what he is really about. I'll talk more about my experience with moving fast later on.

I've learned and noticed that most of us young heads don't really date the right way. It's like you start to deal with someone from around the way and you either start out on the low or open with it. You go out a few times, then y'all have sex and go out some more until someone decides to make it official or until a baby pops up. What we as females don't realize, however, is that guys don't know whether we are truly the one for them that early on. They may say I love you and really mean it, but he isn't in love with you, which means his chances of cheating are high. So what happens is, within a few months of taking each other seriously, other females come out the woodworks. Yes, he made it official with you, but he has *not* cut off the ones before you. Why? Because he still hasn't figured it out yet. I learned this from experience and by listening to wise men and women like Tyrese, Rev Run, Tony Gaskins, and Tionna Smalls. That's why I now know that it's better when we take things slow.

Relationships

"Timing is everything with relationships." —Rashida Jones

Relationships are a lot of work and can be stressful at times. The younger you are, the more difficult they will be, because neither you nor the guy really knows yourself. And that's how relationships fall apart. When you're young, relationships shouldn't be pressured or taken too seriously. How you treat the person is what matters. Be friends with a guy first; get to know him and yourself. Go out have fun and don't take it seriously. You aren't married, so don't go acting like it. If you can save yourself the heartache and tears . . . *do so now!* Females mature faster than males, so it's only natural that you'll get your heart broken. What you'll learn is that lots of people, but mostly men, put on a facade as this great guy who sweeps you off your feet, then three months later you see who he really is. So take your time and get to know a person.

A lot of us jump into relationships or even sexual interactions with guys, then we see who he really is and get upset. That has happened to me twice. The first time was with this dude who was a total joke! He asked me to be his girlfriend, and I said okay. As time went on, I started noticing that he was a straight up liar. I remember it like it was yesterday. He was supposed to pick me up one day from work, and he didn't. I called and didn't get an answer, so the next day he called me, I broke it off. He called my mother and told her his ex-girlfriend died. Sis, only if you knew! I knew he was lying, but I decided to still be friends with him. I waited until I got in front of his family and blew his spot up. They told me that I was the only girl who ever called him out on his lies and bullshit. I could not believe how much of a pathological liar he was.

My most recent relationship was with a guy who was ten years older than me. We met on the 4th, had sex on the 6th, and made it official on the 8th. *Fast fast fast!* Everything was happening faster than I'd ever experienced. We got together in July, in September I was at his brother's wedding, and in November were at each other's family house for Thanksgiving. I just knew he was the "one." He said all of the right things, did all of the right things, showed me things I've never seen, and took me to a sexual ecstasy that I've never felt before. I was seeing sounds and flying high first-class, then *boom!* Turbulence started to hit after three months. Honey! If I didn't learn from the last relationship, God said, "Oh, you're going to learn today!" As Tionna Smalls said in her book *Girl Get Your Mind Right*, the guy I met was his representative. I've never met a guy that put on such a front in my life!

He took care of me financially, investing in my business in the first month of us dating. *But!* He emotionally abused me, which I realized later through watching life coaches and preachers, because of his childhood. What I've learned through prayer, meditation, and my self-love journey is that I always had signs that he wasn't ready and that things weren't right; I just decided to ignore them. I learned that had I taken the time to set boundaries and explain what I would and would not put up with, things could've gone smoother and I would've had less heartache. I learned that I didn't love myself as much as I thought I had. Here it was—a man ten years older than me who had no idea how to treat a rare precious diamond (me). And I was a young twenty-two-year-old thinking I could change him. One thing we *cannot* do, sis, is change people, especially a man. At at his age, he has to want to change his ways on his own. So if a guy you're into isn't what you expect, my best advice is to walk away or just be friends, because you're only going to aggravate yourself. We as females get so hyped up when we think we found the one; we don't give it time. Healthy relationships are ones that are patient. We should take our time getting to know each other instead of rushing. I am still growing and learning not to get hyped up too soon.

I definitely won't sit here and only mention the negatives of my relationships, because that wouldn't be reality. I used to blame the guys for all of the things I went through with them, and yes, it was mostly their fault, but as I've grown I've learned to take responsibility as well, because things only happen when you allow them to.

In my relationships I felt protected, because I was with strong men who were respected. I guess I leaned toward men like that because I wasn't raised with a father, so I wanted that protection. The times I did get to see my father, though, I noticed he was a strong and dominant man. My guys taught me to be strong and not care about what people say, because I was weak in certain areas. Most of all, however, I learned a lot about myself.

Abuse

"He doesn't have to hit you for it to be abuse. He can degrade, humiliate, blame, curse, manipulate, or try to control you. It is still domestic violence."
—Unknown

One thing I know for sure is that abuse does not equal love! If he or she is physically hurting you (pushing, slapping, pinching, mushing), verbally hurting you by calling you all kinds of names (bitch, trick, hoe, fat, skinny, ugly, bald headed), or tells you that you'll never become anyone, you need to leave. That is *not* love. Someone who loves and respects you will never purposely hurt you. At the same time, if you love and respect your partner, you wouldn't abuse him or her in any kind of way, either.

Too many females are so used to being abused that when they get into a new relationship they carry the baggage with them, starting fights and provoking the new person they are with to hit them. Then there is manipulative emotional abuse: this person doesn't hit you or curse at you. This person says and does all the right things to get you open, then turns around and does things that make you question whether they still feel the same way. They used to always answer their phone; now they don't. They reject all of your invitations to see you until you start to think it's your fault or that something is wrong with you. Then when they feel you're getting over them, they go back to how they were in the beginning to what you may think is their "normal" self, then they do it all over again.

When I was in a relationship with a man I loved who emotionally and verbally abused me, it was the worst feeling ever. It was like my Prince Charming did all the right things then *boom*! It all just stopped and left me craving more because I got so dependent on the initial love, attention, and affection. When I least expected it, it went away without any reason as to why. There were times when I had to think about what I was going to say in reply to something he said in a regular conversation, because I knew he had all of these insecurities and anger issues. I remember one time we were at a restaurant having lunch, and he was telling me how he felt about the things going on his life. I was sympathetic, but I'm also a realist, so I explained that most of the things he was talking about were results of the life he chose to live in the streets. He got upset and started saying, "Forget it, you're too fucking bougie to understand. You think you're perfect," and was going on and on. I just sat there, quiet, until he decided to calm down.

That right there isn't being called bitch, slut, or hoe, *but* it is still verbal abuse. A *real* man wouldn't get so angry about facts unless he himself has issues. If I am the woman he loves, why would he speak to me that way? As time continued, things just kept getting out of hand, and I knew that one day I was going to walk away and stay away, and that time came after two years. After feeling down and out, when my self-esteem was at an all-time low, and after I lost weight from stress, I finally put my foot down and left him, realizing that I was too dependent on his love. I was so used to the abuse and wasn't truly in love or happy with myself. And only when you're truly happy with *you* is when you can accept affection without depending on it.

It's also not healthy to abuse your children. I see far too many females verbally abusing their kids—telling them to shut the fuck up, go lay their ass down, calling them stupid or retarded little bitches and niggas. That's abuse too. Don't become a victim! If this is something you're experiencing at home watching your mother or father being abused, try talking to someone close to you—an aunt, an uncle, a friend of the family, someone you can confide in about your feelings so you don't have them bottled up. And if you already are a mother, or when you become one, don't turn your child into a victim whether it's you or the father being the one to treat them that way.

Any sort of abuse shouldn't be tolerated. I have witnessed women I love get physically abused by men they loved or by fathers of their children. Abuse can lead to low self-esteem, depression, suicide, and homicide. A lot of people abuse others because they were abused, or because they aren't happy with themselves deep down or even on the surface. Many women who have children stay in abusive relationships, and I say this: it's one thing to stay because you think you love him but another to have kids involved. If you love your kids, you would never allow them to see such unacceptable behavior. It isn't healthy. Your daughter will feel it's okay to be abused and hurt by men, and your son will feel it's okay to abuse and hurt women.

Leave on the first hit. This is not baseball practice. One strike and he's out. Shut him down at the first verbal insult or threat. Check him one time and one time *only*! You must set examples the very *first* time he steps out of line.

Guys only do what you allow, sis.

Street Dudes

"The streets don't love him like he loves them; he loves the streets more than himself, so he can't love you. —Epiphany Kendell

Sis, when I tell you that this is not a route for you, just like everything else, I am speaking from experience. Nothing good can happen for you or to you but heartache, pain, jail visits, worry, and drama. Not to mention the girls and possible STDs that come along with street dudes, too, because guys with cash attract girls—all kinds of them, especially the ones who will do and have done anything for some money and attention. Do not let him tell you "I don't trust these hoes, babe." Believe he's having unprotected sex with them and most likely doing the same things he does to and for you to them. The streets don't love a dude, and neither do the people out in the streets with him. But your dude loves the streets and everything that comes along with it.

No matter what kind of street dude he is—weed seller, coke or crack dealer, gambler, or stickup kid.

Dealing with street dudes had me in situations like selling crack (to women my grandma knew—women I had no idea smoked crack). I sold to a guy who looked like an undercover cop in a staircase. I was scared as hell, but saying to myself, "This is a part of the game, Piff." I was holding guns in my bag while I hung out with my friends. Dealing with another guy in the streets had me stressed out over the fact he went missing. One day he was at my house laughing and having a good time. The night he went missing, he called and told me he loved me and how he was happy that we'd met then said he was on his way. He never came, and the next day, no call.

Days later, I'm seeing his face on television screens, on buses, and getting calls from investigators. Then I found out that he had a baby on the way and heard rumors that he was using drugs. You just never know who you are dealing with in life, sis, especially when dealing with a guy in the streets. That street life is no joke. It's the devil's playground, and unfortunately these guys love the rush and the rides.

One time I unknowingly brought drugs to Rikers Island, and that right there could've really ruined my life. My ex asked me to bring him a pair of jeans the next time I came to see him, and I did. When I left, he called me to say goodnight and told me what he found, and how he had no idea he had some left in his hiding spot. We laughed about it and I was in shock, but after awhile of thinking about it, reality hit, and I was like, *"Oh, my god!"*

Dating street dudes turned jailbirds is a subject I know way too much about. Sad but true. My first boyfriend has been in and out of jail since I met him when he was sixteen years old. Then in my first serious relationship, my boyfriend went to jail for something he didn't do. I say God knows best, because that was something he needed to humble him. He did two years, and I stayed for a year and a half. I left because he had a girl from around the way coming to see him, and he didn't tell me. I felt betrayed, and you know how females give it up when they know something you don't concerning your man. That's another story.

While I was being faithful, I was taking time away from myself and my goals. Even though I was in love with this guy, I should have reminded myself to love me first, to know I wasn't obligated to drive to the prison three times a week, or to be searched and treated like the inmate I was going to see. If you find yourself in this position, remember: He has to do the time, not you. Don't imprison yourself; you have life to live.

Don't get me wrong, I don't regret being there for him at all, but I do feel like I could've gone to see him much less. Sometimes we girls feel like we are obligated, or we feel we have to prove to him that we're "down ass chicks" or "riders." Let's be clear: being a loyal and "down ass chick" to yourself is what's more important, because nine times out of ten, the one we did the bids for did us dirty before they got locked up, and if he hasn't learned to appreciate you he'll do the same when he comes home. Jail or prison, at times, truly changes a guy for the better, sometimes for the worse, and sometimes they stay exactly the same.

My father was a jailbird. He did years and years in prison. He came home when I was sixteen years old and he had been in prison since I was conceived. It's funny how the type of guys my mom attracted, I subconsciously attracted: street guys and jailbirds. I say subconsciously because my dad was the only street dude I knew of her dealing with at a young age, so how did I attract them as well? Going to visit my ex was routine: work, school, Rikers Island—Rikers Island, work, school. There were crying babies, kids running around in the waiting area, girls being loud and ghetto telling one another their stories about why their man is locked up, what his lawyer said, which correction officers are cool and which ones are mean, sharing and giving insight about one another's situations. I get it. As females being here supporting our men, we need encouragement and someone else who understands, but most of these females make that a lifestyle, thinking it's okay. I look at pictures of my dad and me from the time I was born up until a few years before he came home, all in jail! As I've gotten older, I've realized I do not want that for my child, so I will no longer take a guy who has high chances of getting locked up seriously. I do not want my daughter thinking it's okay to deal with a guy who's in the streets doing illegal things and hanging with the wrong people. And I don't want my son thinking it's okay to be that type of guy.

Dealing with street dudes had me in trap houses with drugs, shotguns, and crack heads my age having cyphers with their pipes like it was weed and a blunt. I was locked up for a whole day and a half—which felt like forever—with my life flashing before my eyes, because I was with a boyfriend and his friend in a car while they were riding dirty with $10,000 plus and a gun in the glove compartment. I didn't know until we got pulled over and locked up. A woman cop in the precinct asked what I was in there for, and because I didn't know, I said a bag of weed. She came back to where my cell was and said, "No, honey. You're in here for a gun charge." Sis, I tell you no lie. *I flipped out!* I was pissed off and scared. I was dreading the phone call I had to make to my mother, because I knew how much it was going to hurt her.

You see, you're not the only one who gets affected when dealing with a guy who isn't good for you. It's easy to get in with a street dude, but it's hard as hell to get away from him. When it's time to leave him, you'll feel like if you walk away you aren't loyal. But what I've learned is that your loyalty lies *with yourself!* Living in the hood, street guys are what we are exposed to, but it's not worth it. The guy who can take you to expensive restaurants, buy you the latest bag and shoes, and has jewelry and labels is not worth it. Nor is the thrill of having a tough guy who's hard to figure out, doesn't chase you, and plays games. If he isn't making his money *legally* doing positive things, or if he isn't showing you he respects you, do not entertain him! Don't get me wrong, even the ones with legal jobs can have baggage too, but chances are higher with a guy in the streets.

Sis, there are guys in school who are into positive things like basketball and football. Give that guy a chance. He may not even be the coolest guy, the flyest guy, and girls may not even pay him any attention, but give yourself a chance by giving him a chance. You may be the girl who has a boyfriend with a regular job, and your friend is dating a street guy who buys her all kinds of stuff, but don't compare your situation to hers. Don't let the flashy things a guy may have make you feel like your guy isn't a good guy because he maybe can't afford it or can't get something you want as fast. I can't tell you who to love and I can't tell you to leave the one you feel you love, but the smartest move to make is to not play a street dude too close Jail and a casket are the only two options guys who love the streets have.

The situation when I went to jail recently happened, and while I was in there, I was talking with the correction officers and other women who were locked up. I was telling them what I had going on for myself, and they were like, "Oh, no. You do not belong here." They were praying for me and telling me God would make a way for me. I told them about my book and how I want to help young women, and as I was speaking I realized that no matter how much I loved that guy, no matter how much he held me down, I had to walk away from him. I couldn't be his lady any longer because I had young women looking up to me, and I refuse to tell you one thing while I'm doing another. So I walked away for myself, but mostly for the young me watching. I love him from afar while he loves the streets up close.

Ride or Die

"A ride or die is a female who loves herself enough to know when to put her foot down to teach a guy how to treat her." —Epiphany Kendell

I want you to be very clear as to what "ride or die" means, because many of us get it twisted. Being a "down ass chick" doesn't mean you stick around after he beats you, after he cheats a million times, after he plays you out, or after he takes your money. It does not consist of you fighting over him. This is not a gangster movie. If you love him, then teaching him how to treat a woman is something you should do.

If you have a boyfriend and he loses his job, you don't make him feel less of a guy because of it. You encourage him to find another or even keep your eye out for other jobs for him. A "R.O.D" encourages her man to do positive things like go to school and stay focused. Do not get it mistaken with being with him when he goes to jail a million times, spending your last bit of money on him for commissary or for all of his needs and wants when he's home.

Being a "R.O.D" does not consist of helping him sell drugs, holding guns, and cooking up work for him. Trust me! If he feels that you should be doing those things for him, you need to walk away and never turn back. When I was doing those things for and with my ex, it didn't seem forced. It just seemed like it was natural, which is not a good thing. A life like that is not normal. If he truly loves and wants to be with you, he will be your "R.O.D." He will work an honest paying job or work to own his own business, so he doesn't risk death or jail.

Games

"Don't listen to what a guy says. Watch what he does and how his friends move."
—Epiphany Kendell

Most guys, young and old, play games. I always knew about it because my mom told me, and my ex from my first relationship put me onto all the game. He taught me how to maneuver when it comes to dudes' thought process and how they play girls out. Guys play games with us because they know we females are emotional and sensitive, and it takes guys longer than us to mature, so that is definitely a factor.

What you should do is just have fun if you're dating. Don't get into anything too serious too fast, meaning sex. It's easier to let go of a guy when you haven't had sex with him. There are guys who will tell you they love you just to get some. There are guys who put on a front like you're the only one so you can trick on them. Then there are guys who game you by having you think you're crazy or that you cause him to ignore you or that you're the problem. There are guys who may make you "wifey" or the "main chick" and have other girls on the side. I'm here to tell you that if a guy likes you, he won't want to have anyone else on the side. Like I said, maturity is a factor. I'm not saying you won't get gamed. Some guys are really good at what they do. What I am saying, which is a main point throughout this guide, is focus on *you.*

I can't front. I used to play games with guys, too. You know, the love them and leave them game. The hurt before you get hurt game. I would let a guy get to know me then cut him off. I always had things going on, so I never had time to sweat a dude. So he'd end up hitting me up more than I hit him up. After a while of getting to know him, I would use the power of my vagina to get him even more caught up. I'd play mind games with them and always have them guessing. What I had to learn the hard way is that anytime we as females open our legs, whether the guy is sweating us or not, we're losing. The power is in having a vagina, *not* in using it. Guys see using their sex as power because they already know we get attached emotionally.

One thing you probably don't think about too much is a female running game on a female. I know some straight chicks that can talk you out of your panties. True story. A female with game can trick a young girl into prostitution, stripping, and trafficking drugs. So watch everybody and everything moving at all times.

Tricking

"If you spend all your money on a guy and he leaves, you have nothing."
—Epiphany Kendell

If you do not listen to anything else I say, you better listen when I tell you this: If you spend all your money on a guy and he leaves, you have *nothing*. Yes, it's worth repeating twice. Do not give or trick your money on a guy, sis. I've seen this happen to so many females and it saddens me. There is a difference between buying your boyfriend something for Christmas, his birthday, or just surprising him once every few months, and letting him come to you like an ATM machine or you doing it to keep him. You give him your last dollar, and yeah, he may make you his number one, but isn't being his only one better, especially if you're giving him your last? I've seen females buy their man Gucci sneakers, Louis Vuitton this and YSL that when the shoes on their feet cost $30. *No, no, hell no!* Sis, believe me, the same shoes or sneakers you're buying him, he's stepping out while wearing with the next girl. Yes, any guy can and does step out, but isn't it worse when you're paying for the next girl to enjoy the view?

I've seen females get a car in their name and can't get a ride on a cold day. I've seen females buying diamond chains and watches when they're rocking CZs. And let's not talk about the females who have their man looking better than her and her kids. *You*, my love, my darling little sister, do *not* want to be any of these females. You do not want to be the female responsible for getting a guy fly to impress the next female. There were females tricking on my ex while he was my man. And best believe, I let someone trick on me right after, and what happened? The world was about to end. Guys are sensitive. But after that, I bet he didn't accept anymore "gifts." Females will do anything to keep or try to get a man; do not be one of the dry throat thirsty ones. *Know your worth!* And not only that, sis, but there are females who stay in crazy situations because their man tricks on them by paying bills, buying them the latest, and spoiling them with lavish gifts. Every woman wants to be spoiled, but at what cost? Why would you stay in a situation where you're being mistreated and or used?

Guys are known to trick on women they like or even women they don't like too much. We love to be taken care of. We like nice things, but do not let the fact that a guy tricks on you allow you to stay in a situation that isn't healthy for you. A lot of guys feel they can talk to you any kind of way and do anything they want, if they feel like they own you.

Sex

"Sex: The thing that takes up the most amount of time and causes the amount of trouble." —John Barrymore

Boy, oh boy! This subject is very touchy because sex can bring you up or bring you down. Great sex can have you feeling like you're on cloud nine, but great sex from a guy who doesn't know your worth will have you sad and depressed and wanting more. Lord knows I know from experience. I learned that we as females won't even experience what real great sex feels like until we're a bit older. When I was seventeen, I thought that what I was feeling while having sex was the shit until I got older. I realize now it was all a waste of time, energy, and my innocence—a female's most precious and sacred piece.

I remember having sex and thinking to myself, *"Now what was the point of that?"* Not because it was wack, but because I didn't even really like the guy. At that time, I knew how to have sex without feelings, and I did it well. I hurt a few guys' feelings because they thought things were going well, but I was bored, so I made them feel special. I gave them a part of me, then didn't want to be bothered anymore. It was wrong of me, yeah, but it was also stupid, because I was wasting time and lowering my stock.

You also need to know, sis, that every time you have sex with someone your value drops. Just like the more kids you have while you aren't married and by different guys, your value drops. So before you have sex for the first time or for the one-hundredth time, think to yourself: Is it worth it? Is he worth it?

One thing about sex that needs to stay on your mind, whether you're having it or thinking of having it, is *protection*! Sex should be saved for marriage, honestly. If I knew how to properly masturbate years ago, I definitely would've held out. Since I know now, that's what I do. But to be real here, a lot of you are probably already having sex (although I want you to completely stop and save yourself from here on out). Unprotected sex should be saved for marriage (if you're already active) because that is when you both are *supposed* to be faithful to each other and are open to having children. Like I said before, when you know better, you do better.

I can't front. I've hurt those who wanted more, but I've also had a reality check dealing with a guy who was just for the sex. I caught myself liking him, so I fell back, because those of us who are smart know that when you get into a situation with a guy and never demand anything more from the jump, that's how it will always be. See, we started out always hanging out at his house with our friends. After awhile, we got physical. From there, anytime I hit him up, it was always for that. I'd never let him hit me up for it, because I felt that I should do what I want, when I want. As time went on, I started to like him because he was different from any guy I dealt with—he was in college, didn't get into any drama, and had a regular job. Husband material to me, but I clearly wasn't what he considered wifey material because I'd ask him to hang out in the city to catch a movie and he wasn't with it. So I had to come to my senses and leave him alone. To him, I was acting funny. To me, I was saving myself the embarrassment I knew was soon to come had I continued. So see, sis, sometimes you have to know what things really are when dealing with guys, even though they don't always say what it really is because they might be afraid of hurting you or don't want you to stop giving them sex. You have to keep your ears and eyes open for signs. They always show their true intentions; it's just up to us to pay attention.

STDs

"Prevention is better than a cure." —Desiderius Erasmus

STDs can and do happen to any and all people— no matter their race, age, sex, social class, weight, or height. What usually happens is that you trust a guy whom you believe loves you enough to let him go raw inside you. What you don't know is that he either has an STD from his last relationship and never got checked and doesn't have any symptoms yet, or he's been going raw in another girl (or girls), knowing he has something and just doesn't care. Now he's dealing with you. Be different! Be safe! Make him wrap it up. I remember dealing with a guy I loved and going to the doctor to get a checkup only to find out he gave me an STD. I was livid. I couldn't believe it! *"Me? Now way! How could this happen? I wasn't sleeping around . . . Duh, Piff. It happened when you decided to have unprotected sex with a guy without making him get checked like you've been doing since you started having sex."* That's what the voice in my head said to me as I was sitting in the OB/GYN office.

You would think that stopped me from doing it again. Nope! I dealt with someone else I trusted years later, only for the same thing to happen again. My family doctor said to me with the screwface, "Do you not know how to say no? Are you looking to get HIV/AIDS? Do you not love yourself? Not even certain husbands are trustworthy enough." All I could do was cry.

because he was right for speaking to me like that. The questions he asked were questions I asked myself before. It was clear that I did not love myself at all. A few guy associates I know who sleep around protect themselves more than females in relationships.

Listen, sis. It's not a good feeling physically or emotionally, so save yourself the trouble and heartache. Do not think it can't happen to you, because it can and will if you aren't safe. Even if you read my story and say, "Yo, she's stupid." *Great*! Now be and do better than me. My situation where the guy was clearly having unprotected sex with me and another female could've led to a serious situation. He didn't know whether or not I was having unprotected sex with someone else and she could've been doing the same. The fact that he didn't care about his life, her life, or mine made me say, "Wow, Piff. You really don't know this person." People are capable of anything, and that's how sad situations like HIV and herpes, which you can't get rid of, happens to people who think they can trust someone else with their life.

It's also important to know that several STDs don't always come with symptoms, especially in men. So if they're feeling fine, they might think everything's okay, but if they're not getting tested they don't know. Make sure you're getting tested frequently, especially if you're sexually active, even if you're using protection. Even when I use protection or go through my celibate stages, I get scared when I get tested because of the mistakes of not using protection that I made in the past. It's scary because it takes six weeks to *six months* after you have unprotected sex for a test to detect HIV. Most STDs can be detected two weeks after, so don't just run out the next day to get tested; get tested regularly. Don't be naive and think it can't happen to you, sis, because it can! Wrap it up, be safe, and get tested.

If it's happened to you before, just be smarter now. It's not worth it. If he doesn't want to wrap it up, you as a smart young woman should wrap that situation up by walking away. I want you to know that you aren't alone—unfortunately, STDs are common. I remember feeling alone when it happened to me because I knew my friends at that time couldn't relate, but they were very supportive. As I've gotten older and began talking to other female friends who have been through things, I opened up and realized I wasn't the only one, which also helped them realize they weren't the only one. Many of my guy friends have experienced it at least once, same with my girlfriends. Having friends who support is beautiful, but having friends who support you and can relate make you feel so blessed and at ease. You are not alone, believe me!

And listen, if you are a girl with an incurable STD like HIV/AIDS, herpes, or HPV, do not let that get you down. Life still goes on and God knows best. You may think no one will love, respect, or adore you enough to be with you, but that's not true. That's the devil messing with your insecurity, trying to break you down. Keep your faith, eat right, do things that make you happy, and focus on God, your dreams, and your goals. When the time is right, the one for you will appear. There is someone for everyone.

Stand for something or fall for anything!

Abortions

"Abortions are never an easy thing to do, but if you have to do it, by all means do it." —Epiphany Kendell

Having an abortion is one of the hardest things a girl can go through. I swear I wish I had not even put myself in a situation where I felt forced to have one. And to think that there are females out there who use abortion as a form of birth control, going to get an abortion every time they get pregnant instead of using protection. That isn't good for your body, because when you are ready to have a baby, there is a good chance you won't be able to carry it. When I found out I was pregnant, I was so scared. The first thing on my mind was, "I am getting rid of this." I remember that moment clearly. I felt like my life was going to be over, and that's because my subconscious self knew that there was more to life for me than being a young mother. I sat in my room and thought: "Okay, if I keep this, how am I going to change my room around? What do I have to offer a child? As a twenty year old with no real life experience, what can I teach a child about life? Do I want to grow up with my child or help my child grow up?"

I was working at the Gap as a sales associate making $9.75 an hour—hardly enough to take care of myself, let alone a baby. But I knew I had the best support system anyone could ask for: my mother, my grandmother, and the would-be father's mom. The would-be father wasn't on that list because he was young and I knew that if I did keep my baby, I would have to look at it as mine. If he decided to play his part, then so be it, but I wasn't counting on it. Me being who I am, I could never depend on others to fully help me.

When I told my mom, she was totally disappointed in me. She couldn't believe I had gotten myself into this situation—not just the pregnancy but the whole unprotected sex thing. She is all for abortions if you aren't far along, so that's what I did: for my future and for all of the sacrifices my mom made for me as a young single mother.

On the bed at my doctor's office, at first, I was really nonchalant and cool about everything. When she did the sonogram to see how far along I was, I was curious to see. She asked if I was sure, and I said yes. When I saw that little egg shape on the screen, I was like *"Wow!"* I felt excitement and hurt all at the same time. At that moment, I wished I hadn't asked to see. She stuck some pills inside me vaginally and gave me some pills to take orally. The aftereffect was crazy! I actually had to go back again because the entire fetus wasn't out of me; I was sick physically, emotionally, and mentally. I went on for awhile being extra sad when I saw babies, thinking about what mine would have looked like and how my life would've been.

When I went to church and confessed what I had done out loud was when I finally let go and let God. I felt a full sense of relief. To actually hear myself say what I had done in front of people I didn't really know and for them to tell me it was okay and that God forgave me was exactly what I needed.

A few days later, I found out that the guy I was pregnant by had a girl who he'd been dealing with for a while pregnant at the same time as me. I did the math and we would've been in labor about a week apart. That made me a bit relieved about my decision because that would've been a real Maury Povich situation. Who wants to walk around with a baby who has a sister or brother the same age with different mothers?

Abortions are never an easy thing to do, but if you have to do it, by all means do it. If it's something you don't believe in or feel as if you can't do, *do not* get yourself into any situations that will get you pregnant—*point blank!* There are many forms of birth control if you are choosing to have sex. Besides condoms, there are the ring, the patch, the shot, and the pill, which I am sure you know. I have tried every last one, and the one that works best for me is the pill, but if you know you aren't responsible enough to remember to take it, get the Depo shot. You only have to get it every three months. And if you are on birth control, it does *not* mean you shouldn't use protection. Getting infected with HIV or herpes is a lifelong and incredibly tough situation to be in and can only be prevented by using condoms.

Young Mothers

"Yes, you are a young mom. No, your life isn't over" —Epiphany Kendell

Yes, sis, babies are beautiful blessings, but having them at a young age really isn't the smartest move, especially for a girl in the hood living with her family (You know these apartments are shoebox small). Wouldn't you want the whole experience of having your own place and your baby having its own room? Even if you had a one-bedroom apartment before you got pregnant, the fact that it's yours is what makes the difference. It's said that we females don't know who we are until thirty years old. Our twenties are when we make the most mistakes, and our teen years are for us to be young and immature. If you are still a baby yourself, why would you have one? If you have one already, there's obviously nothing you can do. But I would suggest that you use protection. With being a young mother of one, you can still move around much more freely. You can accomplish your goals without too much pressure, and to keep it real it's easier and cheaper to find someone to watch one child.

Babies are a full-time job, and once you have one, life is no longer fully about you. if you're young, living at home, and still figuring life out, do all that you can do to keep yourself from getting pregnant. Ask yourself:

What do you have to offer a baby?

What can you, as a young mom still experiencing life teach a child?

Can you afford a child?

What if the father leaves? Will you be emotionally strong?

If you had no help from anywhere, would you be okay with that?

If the government stopped helping, would you survive?

Most times, if it's not because she wasn't allowed to have an abortion or because she couldn't afford to have one in time, females have a baby to keep a dude around. It's so sad! There are those of us who fall victim to having a baby because we feel we're in love, and because the guy wants one. I've been there before, twice! I was in love and not using protection because deep down I knew he wanted me to have his baby; and I felt he was the one. I felt like, "Wow, he loves me that badly that he wants me to have his baby; he wants to keep me around." Thank goodness I didn't get pregnant. God knew it wasn't my time and that neither of those guys were the one for me. Guys sometimes fall in love with the thought of you. I say that because they think, "Here's this girl who is ambitious, pretty, dresses nice, and doesn't sweat me. I need to trap her down." I since dealt with a few guys who told me that I am "baby mother material."

I felt insulted because I always knew, and still do know, that I am "wife" material. I know that I am worth way more than what the average hood guy who doesn't know his own worth has to offer me. If he can make you the mother of his child, he can make you his wife. *Point blank!* But *boys* know nothing about that, because they know nothing about themselves. I know so many females who have nothing going for them and end up having a baby, thinking the father will treat them better. And if he does treat you better, why would you want to be with him, knowing he's only doing that because you have his kid?

I know females who have a baby because the dude has a job and is getting money, is "known" around the way, or has "good hair." Females who never had much growing up use having a baby by a certain dude as what they feel is a "come up." All the while the father isn't around during the whole pregnancy, or if he is, it's for his benefit, and girls allow this to happen because they just want that "family" feeling anytime they can get it. This situation locks a woman into feeling or being totally dependent on the man, whether or not he's dependable. It's not good for anyone involved, including the child. There are also the girls who have the father of their child denying it or not wanting it, then as soon as you have the baby, he wants to be around. Okay, granted, he's the father—he needs to be around, too, for his child; but you, as a young woman, should never allow him back in between your legs again. Or at least give it a full year or so to see how he treats you and your child. Do not make a big decision too soon. Please, sis, do not be one of the females who feel, because they've traveled (or visited Miami once) and clubbed a few times, they've lived life (because you haven't).

A lot of the time, it's a cycle: the mother had kids at a young age, so the daughter has a kid at a young age. If that's all you're exposed to and no one is showing you otherwise, that's what happens; you conform to the norm. They don't have people around them showing them that life is bigger than having a baby young and putting your life on hold. I also feel that a lot of young women want to be mothers to have someone to love or because everyone else is doing it. I hear girls saying everything happens for a reason, that God planned for this to happen. I agree with God having a plan, but let's be serious. Anytime you have unprotected sex, the chances are high that you'll end up pregnant. If you aren't using birth control, you will get pregnant. That's not God! That's you being careless. If you were always using condoms and it broke, or you were on birth control and you still got pregnant, that would be God's plan; that happened for a higher reason.

But just because you have one doesn't mean your life is over or that you have to forget about yourself. Here is my take on being a young mother: when you find out you are pregnant and decide to keep it, school and work should be the first things you think about. Far too many young mothers get lazy and dependent solely on the government for assistance. Then you have those who feel like because their man hustles or has a little job that they don't have to work, which, to me, is far more stupid than depending on the government. Snap out of la la land! When you have a child, it's not up to your grandmother, mother, or the child's grandmother on the father's side to raise *your* child. Because you want to act your age now and run around outside all hours of the night, you think leaving your child home is right?

For those who can't leave the baby at home, do you think running around with your baby stroller housing you and your friend's liquor bottles at the bottom of it is right? Do you think you should have someone watching your child while you hang out on the block doing nothing? While you hang out in the basketball court doing nothing? Rather than being out doing nothing, you can be home giving your baby a bath and putting him or her to sleep at a proper time. At the same time, you can be relaxing, studying, reading a book, reading parenting magazines and learning something, and thinking of ways to better your life. I'm not saying you can't have a life, but you have to play your number one role first, and that's mommy. I see a lot of girls who would rather buy hair weave, shoes, and clothes than to spend money on diapers and baby wipes. I see girls who know that people feel sorry for them, so they feel they don't have to buy anything for their child, because others will do it for her.

Don't be the young mother who has a baby and then keeps having them—that's not cute. You aren't married, and you're living at home sharing a room with your kids and your baby father; that isn't cute. And if that is you, sis, go hard with school and work. Do what you have to do to get out of that cramped-up space. Kids need space to play, to grow, and to be kids. Having kids by every guy you sleep with isn't cute either. And, sis, if you are not sure who the father of your child is, you need to be real with yourself, as well as the guys you were sleeping with. Do not have a guy thinking a child is his when you aren't sure; it is not right! That is a serious situation and no one should walk around thinking they have a child in this world when they don't. If there are too many guys to choose from and you feel you want to have the baby, woman up and take your Ls (your losses), and keep it moving. These are the choices you made, so you have to live with them and make the best of them.

Baby Daddies and Baby Mamas

"Make sure she respects your position, and make sure you you respect hers."
—Epiphany Kendell

As a young woman with no kids, this subject is very serious for me because it is hard to wrap my mind around being with a guy who has a kid. I am not one of those females who thinks, "Oh no, if he has kids, I can't deal with him." *But!* I do think twice, and I pay even closer attention to situations like this. My only time dealing with a guy who had a kid, I wasn't threatened at all by his child's mother. Anytime she called, it was always about their child; he'd even put her on speaker. I respected him for trying to reassure me that there was nothing going on between them, but I wasn't really worried because I knew anything that happened with his baby mama would come out quicker than him cheating with a random chick.

Some guys have to realize that if they know their child's mother is a bird head (immature), he has to put her in her place from the time he feels he no longer wants to be with her. If proper communication isn't established, when the next female (you) comes into his life, there is going to be lots of drama, and who wants to deal with that, especially at a young age? Females (and males) feel that because they have a child with someone that they own that person. If they are still having sex with each other while they both have someone else, that is what makes me stand clear of the baggage, as should you. Especially if you, her, and him live in the same neighborhood. I've learned that it's not good to shit where you eat, which means do not date someone from your neighborhood.

If you are dealing with a dude who has a kid, make sure you are asking him lots of questions and being very clear as to what you will not tolerate. Baby mamas will try you, whether she is a bird head or not! It may not even be about you. It could be that she wants to see if she still has a hold on him, or she's mad that he's treating you better than he treated her after all that she has put up with. Just make sure she respects your position, and make sure you you respect hers. A lot of females who deal with a dude with a situation like this tend to get jealous of the child's mother, especially if he isn't beefing with his child's mother. It's like, *calm down.* If you have him now, there is clearly something that wasn't right between them. Be secure about yourself and your position in his life. Besides, the last thing you want is for them to be beefing, because it will stress him out and put a strain on the relationship you have with him.

If you are the baby mother, *do not* be the one who won't let go! Get yourself together and stop chasing and worrying about what he's doing or if he's with the next chick. You no longer have yourself to think about anymore. You have a child, so focus on you and her or him. *Do not* be that chick that feels like, "Oh, I put all of these years in, went through all of this drama, I'll be damned if I let him go." *Cut it out!* Yes, you might have gone through a lot with him—jail bid, him cheating, holding him down with your income tax checks for a re-up for drugs, etc.—but listen, baby girl, you decided to do that! And we all know that when you give him your all and he decides to leave, you have nothing! Older women always tell me, "You have a choice of who the father of your child is; make sure you choose right."

Breakups

"Some people think it's holding on that makes one strong; sometimes it's letting go." —Unknown

Heartbreak is one of the things we all experience, males and females. I remember my first heartbreak. I actually caused it myself, as I often do. I was confused about being with him, so I broke up with him. We were in the ninth grade and I remember it like it was yesterday. He started dating someone else but always hinted to me that when I was ready to be with him I should let him know. Me being me, I didn't speak up, but I wanted him back so bad! He wouldn't come back unless I told him to though. My pride is something I am still working on to this day. So I had to see him and hear about him being with other females, and it tore me apart!

My first young heartbreak that was caused by the guy was when I found out my then-boyfriend was messing around with a girl from around my way. My first-ever *real* heartbreak was a double hitter: it was when a "friend" at the time told me over Facebook that the man I was madly in love with tried to holla at her three months before. I was devastated and heartbroken by these two people I loved so much. I was heartbroken by her because as a friend she should've told me face-to-face when it happened, and I was heartbroken by him because he was the first guy I loved that hard. She was the friend I'd kill for, if anyone tried to hurt her; he was the one I'd walk across broken glass that was set on fire for. So, see, you can be heartbroken by a friend as well as someone you're dating.

Breakups are never a pretty or easy thing to do, especially when years and lots of time together have been invested. Sis, when you're in your teens, you feel like three months is forever, but as you grow, you will see how time flies and how precious it is. I haven't had many breakups because I haven't had many serious relationships, but the breakups I've endured have always been really nerve-racking and emotional. The worse on-and-off breakup I experienced wasn't in my teens. It was actually in my twenties, with an ex who I was sprung off of, meaning I was blinded by good sex and charm. I am not saying love didn't eventually grow, but the foundation wasn't built off of it, which is why things didn't work out. Every time we broke up, I felt free but also missed being needed and wanted. So even if things weren't the way I wanted them to be, I'd settle for it because the sex was good, he held me down financially when I had a job and when I didn't, and because of the emotional dependency I had.

The breakups in my teen years weren't that bad because I was young and hadn't put much energy into the relationships. It was different being a bit older, dealing with an older guy, because he knew a bit more as far as manipulation and game. He knew when and how to take full control; he watched and learned me. What got me over my breakups from a young age until now and allowed me to become stronger is the fact that I always had things going on—work, school, side projects. So my mind would be focused on more important things.

But don't get me wrong, I'm human. I went through all of the stages of a breakup. The sleepless nights, turning stomach, heart dropping, weight loss, no appetite, thoughts of that person, wishing they'd call, depression, and everything else that comes along with it. Oh gosh, I remember each one like it was yesterday! I went through all of the stages of a breakup. The sleepless nights, turning stomach, heart dropping, weight loss, no appetite, thoughts of that person, wishing they'd call, depression, and everything else that comes along with it.

The thing about dealing with someone around your way is that you'll have to see him or her and hear about whom they're with after you and possibly see them with that person. It's also difficult to heal when you're still going over to his family's house or still talking to his friends; you have to cut everyone connected to him off until you are completely over him. With my recent ex, I didn't have to see him or who he was dealing with because he lived out of town. But it was still hard, because any time he'd call, I'd go running. Anytime he texted, I responded. And when he didn't hit me up, I'd hit him up to see what he was doing, which I already knew would end in him telling me he loved me and so on. But when he acted up, we would break up again and I'd go back to the symptoms of heartbreak.

What I can say, sis, is that it gets better and better as time goes on. Your mind gets used to it and you become immune. But what you don't want to do is become so immune to the point where you keep going back because you think you can handle it. The point is to get strong enough to walk away and stay away, but do *not* beat yourself up about falling back into him when you do. Life is about falling and getting back up, but do not allow it to drag you down. There are many situations where a couple has been on and off a lot and then finally get together for good, but most of the time it's just a waste of time and energy. Besides, when you're young, fixing a relationship should be the very *last* thing you should be worried about. To lift myself up, I change my hairstyle, paint my nails, go through my closet and switch my style up, and hang out with my girls. Basically, I do things that make me feel better, things that lift me up. I've always been this way, thanks to my mother and grandmother. There are times I feel alone, which is mostly at night when I'd prefer to have someone to talk to about nothing and hear the constant *I love you*. Then I'd have to say to myself, "Piff, you felt alone and unappreciated most of your relationship, from him not being there how you needed him to be. You felt alone when he'd rather give you money instead of time and loyalty, so what's the difference now that you aren't with him?" Then I would continue doing things that made me happy and lifted me up. There were times he'd ask to take me out and if I wasn't busy I would, and I'd only go when I was feeling great enough to shut him down if he tried to make a move. I felt like as long as I wasn't giving him my body I was winning, because I wouldn't get so wrapped up in my feelings and emotions. There are times I would think I couldn't wait, until I didn't even want to hang out with him anymore. That day finally came when the dust settled and the wars finally ended.

The things about heartbreak is that it hurts real bad when it first happens, but somehow your heart gets stronger from it, and you learn to deal with situations better. My feelings have been hurt numerous times in different situations that occurred with guys I've dealt with, but I always bounce back better than before. That's what you have to do: stay strong, love yourself, stay on top of your game, and *stay busy*! The busier you are, the less time you have to think about the situation that hurt you. I'm not saying you won't feel it. It's okay to cry. Crying helps a lot by allowing you to release the stress. Do not let anyone make you feel like crying is weak, because it's not—it helps a lot. I used to be like, "I feel stressed, I feel bottled up, I need to cry." I pay close attention to my feelings.

Breakups and Friends

It's important that you are there for your friends who goes through breakups, because girls need girls to lift one another up. We need one another to let each other know, "Listen, boo. You're too good for him. Let's go get some ice cream because stressed spelled backwards is desserts." It's hard being there for a friend, though, who goes through a breakup with a guy who clearly doesn't respect her. My advice for you: be the friend who's always there and listen, but do *not* give advice after the one hundredth time. If after the first fifty times she doesn't get it, she'll either never get it or she'll get it on her own time.

So don't stress yourself out. I remember being there for someone every time she went through it with her no-good man, and she'd turn around and be right back with him. After a while, I just started not to care and got to the point where she knew not to even mention him, because I was done! I was done seeing her cry over the same thing all the time, I was tired of hearing her say what she was going to do and how she knew he is her downfall, then seeing her go back to him. I feel like, personally, there is no way you can love yourself if you keep going back to someone who treats you like shit.

That's the hard part about caring for friends so much: when she's hurt, you hurt, so you step in her shoes and start to feel for her and want to make every move for her. Not every female is as strong as the next, but you have to have some kind of sense of what's acceptable and what's not. I've been there for friends who went through breakups (as they were for me, every and *all of the time*) and not because their guy was a dog, but because, like every guy, he had to learn his lesson. And when I'm giving advice, I think about both sides when talking to a friend, and I let her know that if she goes back, she should make sure she's going back for the right reasons.

Exes

"Forget what hurt you, but never forget what it taught you." —Unknown

Whether my ex-boyfriends or my ex-friends, everyone has played an important part in my life, and no matter what they may have done that I felt was grimy or wrong, I don't regret having them in my life. I am at a place in my life where I can now look at situations and say, "You know what? I may have had a part in the reason they are no longer in my life" or "That needed to happen so that we could see and learn a lesson." I can't say that I won't have relations with anyone from the past, because only God has the answers. I am a firm believer in people being called an ex something for a reason. Please believe, before I make anyone an ex, they did numerous things to me before I walked away for good. I also realize that everyone from the past was growing just as I was; humans make mistakes.

Before you dead situations or even allow people back into your life, ask yourself:

Does this person bring happiness into my life?

Do I laugh more than I cry because of this person?

Is this person loyal?

Can I trust this person?

Can I be me around this person without them bad-mouthing me later?

Is this person worth a seat in my life again?

Was the situation serious enough for me to cut them off?

I have cut people off for stupid reasons, and I've accepted people back into my life after they've done foul things to me when I shouldn't have, so now I watch people's character closely.

Worth

"When your self-worth goes up, your net worth goes with it."
—Mark Victor Hansen

Your self-worth will determine how far you get in life. If you do not know your worth, you will not be respected. Growing up, I knew my worth to a certain extent. When boyfriends cheated, I would leave and then take them back when I thought they learned their lessons. (I say "they" because clearly I was dating guys who weren't finished being players.) But there comes a time, which should be when you're first dating someone, when you have to let them know what you will and will *not* accept, and stick by your word

Do not become one of those older women who are with the same person for years and years, crying and complaining about how her partner doesn't treat her right. Trust me! So many women settle for less, not knowing their worth or knowing and just putting it to the side so they won't be lonely.

Do not settle for less with someone because you do not want to be lonely, because he's paying your bills, or because he's buying you nice things. I also know women who settle for less from a man who does absolutely nothing for her but stress her out! When you learn to love yourself, you will not accept less than the best or put up with disrespect from a guy. Although a guy really never played me out as far using me, cursing me out, or calling me names like stupid or bitch, I played myself by having sex "like a dude." That was proof that I didn't know my worth. *Girls who know their worth run the world!*

If he would rather hang with his friends and only wants to hang with you when it's good for him, he doesn't think you're worthy. If he never makes time to take you on dates but has time to fuck you when he wants, he doesn't think you're worthy. If he never picks up your call but expects you to pick up when he calls, he doesn't think you're worthy. If you tell him the things you like to do and he never offers to do them with you, he doesn't think you're worthy. I'm not talking about expensive things either. If he knows he's man enough to want sex, he should know you are woman enough—even if a young woman—to like flowers and chocolate just because.

Far too many of us females let guys slide, so when he gets to the next female—which could mean you or me—those of us who know our worth have to check them at the door, just so they'll know we don't play that. What gets me even more livid is when females play the side chick role, they say every guy cheats (which I do not agree with). If all females knew their worth and respected themselves, though, who would the guys have to cheat with? Do not deal with a guy who you know has a girlfriend. It's so classless and trashy! Do not be a dude's second option. Why be the girl he calls after he calls the one he loves? Why accept the doggy bag when you could've been there eating?

I know so many females who were sitting waiting for my boyfriend and I to break up just so they could be seen walking with him. I *never* knowingly played sideline—that's something I did not play with. If anything, I always had a boyfriend who was young and dumb and who had side chicks, and whenever I found out about them, I left him until he learned his lesson. That's one thing about me. The guys I've dealt with always said that I was quick to walk away. You're damn right! I may have played dumb a few times in my relationships, but all in all, I got my respect and my point across about my worth and I've grown to know it more. Anytime I walked away from a situation because I felt I wasn't being treated right, when I did allow the guy to come back, he always came back correct. I do not and you should not allow a guy to call you "my bitch," "my nigga," or any other street names that he may call his friends. I do not even allow my guy friends to talk to me like that. To some it may not be serious, but to me it is.

Knowing your worth doesn't only pertain to relationships. You have to know your worth in every aspect of life: in friendships, business relations, and at work. When you are out in the world working hard for a promotion and you know you are being overlooked, it's up to you to bring it to your boss. It's up to you to speak up when it gets to the point when you can't take it. You have to take your talents and your worth and go somewhere that will recognize worth and more. As far as friendships are concerned, you have to know that when you are being a good friend to someone and they don't appreciate you or what you bring, let it be known—and if the person doesn't fix it, walk away. Only you know your worth, and it's up to you to show other people how to treat you.

Drama

"Negative people need drama like oxygen; stay positive, it will take their breath away." —Unknown

Drama is for those who aren't happy with themselves or their life. To them, drama is like air they need to survive; they live off of it. I hear about the drama going on around me and I can't help but shake my head. In my opinion, people love the drama, because the reasons for it can always be avoided. It seems to *always* be about some girl who slept with another woman's baby father who she's still with, someone's husband, or he-say, she-say. That's simple common sense right there. For one, do not sleep with a guy you *know* has a girlfriend, wife, or baby mother he still deals with. Two, do not gossip with people who aren't your close friends. I always hear about a female having to step to another female because of gossip. That's all unnecessary drama brought on by one's own self.

As far as my experiences, the drama I've had has always been about work stressing me out, an ex-boyfriend being stupid, or me doing dangerous things with an ex or on my own. There's never been drama from outside sources, unless someone was straight up hating for no reason. Rise above it; do not fall victim to it. When people say, "Oh, that's life," I tell them *"No, the hell it's not!"* Life, as I've said before, is what you make it out to be. So if your life is full of drama, that's what you want and like. Honey, if you like it, I'll stay far away from you, because I am not about that life!

Boredom

"Boredom is either what spurs bad decisions or any at all." —Amy Seimaz

They say boredom kills, and in the hood that's *real talk*! I've heard so many stories of how fights just started up out of nowhere between girls and guys. "Idle time makes for the devil's playground." I know you heard that before. If you're home doing something productive or somewhere out in the nearest city or downtown area discovering something new, or doing something productive, there wouldn't be any drama for you to get into. My old crew and I use to get $20 and borrow a metro card and go straight to the city *every time* we were bored, or go hang out at a friend's studio with our B&J cooler drinks in water bottles. Anything beats just hanging around the hood doing nothing with the same people.

I remember being so bored I'd call guys I wasn't interested in to talk or maybe even hang out with, which would make them think I was into them, then I'd end up ignoring them. Or I'd call up an ex, which only brought old drama, old feelings, and flashbacks.

It's better to stay as busy as possible at all times, even if you're reading a book or magazine.

Books

"A room with no books is like a body without a soul." —Marcu Tullius Cicero

Reading is fundamental. There is nothing like a smart girl from the hood: street smart and book smart. What more could a guy or the working world ask for? The thing is, so many of us have our head stuck in these hood novels, because there's drama in there that we can relate to—drug dealers, flyy guys, Rikers Island, baby mama drama, pretty girls, cat fights over guys, family issues, shopping, sex. Why read something you can clearly walk outside and see, hear about, or deal with in your own life? When I was in the seventh and eighth grade, I read those books, and as I got older that's what I was attracted to in my life. We must learn to feed our minds with more than that. It's okay to read those kind of books once in awhile for pleasure, but more often you should be reading books that will make you smarter and more advanced.

The early bird gets the worm, so if you're up on something early, you'll get the rewards from knowing. There is nothing like going somewhere out of the hood and being able to talk about a certain kind of book or situation with people who wouldn't even expect you to be up on it. It feels so good to me *every time*! I have never liked being places and not being able to speak about different topics and situations that were going on around the world. Take pride in knowing things, reading up on different topics, and educating yourself. If you want to learn a new language, buy or borrow books from the library that teach you. If you want to learn how to save and balance your money, look for books that help you do that. Two of my favorites are *Rich*

Dad, Poor Dad and *Think and Grow Rich.* If fashion is your dream, then you should be up on every fashion magazine and book. If cooking is your passion, you should be investing in cooking literature and travel food magazines.

Education

"An investment in knowledge pays the best interest." —Benjamin Franklin

Knowledge is power and knowledge is attractive. Educating yourself by exploring, asking questions, trying new things, experiencing different cultures and foods, and listening to different types of music are all things you can do to educate yourself. School is very important and graduating high school is a major accomplishment. I myself obtained my GED, which isn't bad, but if you have the opportunity to say you actually graduated— take it! I say college is *vital* because of today's economy. At the same time, there are many people who have succeeded without a college degree because of their talent, drive, and ideas. It all depends on what you want to accomplish in life.

I felt that college wasn't for me, but I made sure to go to a bookstore every day after or before work and on the weekends to read up on everything and all things that I was interested in. I am proud of my small collection of books that I acquired during my days at the bookstore. There were times when I would spend my last bit of money on fashion magazines and business books. I take pride in being able to speak about certain situations and topics in an articulate manner. The times I could've been hanging out, I decided to educate myself. I worked as an intern for free at AKOO and Blac Label—that was me educating myself, and the fact that I got to hang out in VIP sections at the hottest clubs made it even better (I'll discuss more of that later).

Don't get me wrong: I went to Katharine Gibbs, a private fashion college. I went to learn how to sew, because I thought I wanted to be a fashion designer. After I realized that wasn't what I wanted to do, I left. Then I attended Berkeley College for fashion merchandise and marketing. It was fun, but I was bored in the classes and realized that wasn't what I wanted either. Today, I finally know what I want to go to school for, and I pray to God it works out for me.

One thing you have to know, sis, is that *knowledge is power*! When you know better, you do better. The better you do things and the more you know, the more money you can make. The more money you make, the more you can help those in need. That's what life's about: learning, growing, succeeding, and helping others learn, grow, and succeed.

Mentorship

"In learning you will teach, and in teaching you will learn." —Phil Collins

Mentorship is very important to me because it helped me get to where I am today, in addition to my aunt, stepdad, and my mother always pushing, supporting, and telling me I can do whatever I put my mind to. I have women from different backgrounds who I look to for advice about certain things. When I went through breakups, I'd reach out to one of my mentors who knows the game, which is her strong point, so she'd give me the proper advice. When an STD situation happened, I went to a mentor who I know experienced the same thing, because I knew I'd get the advice and support I needed. My mother is someone I go to all the time, because I know she's my rock. I am the type of person who needs to hear other people's opinion to see things from a different perspective. And that is what life is about: learning, listening, and being able to get information from different people who care for your wellbeing, so you can sum it all up and make the move you feel is right for your life's journey.

Find a mentor who has qualities that you would like to have as you grow into the person you want to be. It can be a teacher at your school who has a positive outlook on life, a neighbor with style and class, or even someone like Oprah. Although you don't know her personally, you can always watch her interviews to get an idea of where her mind is. I look up to Kimora Lee Simmons because she's fashionable, she's a boss, she has a hood personality, and she's a mother on top of everything she does. She has a lot of qualities that I want to grow to have.

I do not know her personally either, but I have watched her for so long that I have learned a lot from her. I picked out things I liked about her and used them to my advantage in my life. I also have had male mentors, like my stepfather and my uncle, who is also an author. I love them both dearly and respect their opinions.

Church

"Everything we need to know, answers to questions we have, are all in the bible."
—Epiphany Kendell

I speak on church, not to try to convert you if you aren't into God or Christianity, but to tell you how it has helped me, and still does, at times when I've been sad, depressed, or just confused. God's word has helped me through so much. I first started seeking him when I came back to New York City after a sad situation happened to an ex-boyfriend of mine. I was consistent with going to church every Sunday. There were times when I'd party all week and on Saturday, and still get up on time to go to church because I needed to hear God's word. I was about seventeen years old and into church on my own. My mom is Muslim and so is my dad, but they feel that as long as I am serving God, a higher power, they don't care that I'm not Muslim.

Being in church not only helped me in terms of the word of God, but I adopted a new family including church sisters whom I love like my own blood at a great church around my way. Although I eventually stopped attending church on the regular and do not speak to them as much, they are always there when I need advice. When I go back to church after not going for a while, I am embraced and sincerely missed and shown love; it makes me feel great. Sis, no matter where you are, if you are lost with words, confused, or need someone to talk to, go to church and seek God's word. Try it out. I promise you won't regret it. Everything we need to know, answers to questions we have, are all in the bible. Every time I read it, I wonder why I didn't fully seek and listen before. But since you have that chance right now, sis, do so!

Dreams

"All our dreams can come true, if we have the courage to pursue them."
—Walt Disney

Do not let your current situation stop you from following your dreams, whatever they may be. Living in the hood, I know when you hear that, you tend to think, "Yeah, right! That's something the rich say just to say." But I am here to tell you right now: it's the truth! Life is what you make it. *Chase your dreams!* As I am writing this book, I am meeting and seeing more and more people chase their dreams and become successful, which is making me push harder. I was pondering on this book idea with my mom for a long time, and as I am writing I think to myself, "Are you being too open, Piff? How will people react? Are you ready for the criticism? Are you really going to finish this?"

I ask myself those same questions all the time, but I know in my heart this will be worth it. I am going to follow my dreams even if they scare me, even if people criticize me. Because where I am from, not enough people follow their dreams, and I see the result of that. So I follow mine and see how far they can get me. Follow yours to see how far yours can get you.

Acting

I always dreamed of being an actress, so I decided to sign up to act in a play at the neighborhood community center. It was a play about Kwanzaa, and I played Kujichagulia which means self-determination. I was so scared and I messed up on some words, but I kept going. No, it wasn't Broadway or a

Hollywood movie, but it was a chance at my dream, and although after that I decided acting wasn't for me, at least I attempted to follow what was then my dream.

Modeling

When I decided that I wanted to be a model, my mother paid for me to go to modeling school until I felt that wasn't what I wanted to do. But through the classes I learned so much about etiquette: how to walk, how to pose, how to apply makeup, how to clean my face properly. Fast-forward to recently: I tried modeling again, this time some bathing suit pictures that I posted on *Black Men Magazine* online. I realized I was too skinny for that market, but it was so much fun seeing myself in a different light.

I was excited about having friends and family go online to vote for me, and although I wasn't on any magazine pages (since I didn't really pursue that), I enjoyed the shoots and I also enjoyed putting them on Facebook for friends and family to see. Then I went to open castings for a few top agencies, which I realized I had too much meat for. It was all great while it lasted, and I am blessed to have had my mother there with me each and every time at each and every event to support me. I started off on Model Mayhem and met some photographers on there to get my pictures taken, and I styled the shoots myself. I then created a Model Mayhem profile and met better photographers. I started meeting makeup artists, other stylists, and other models. That's how you can get your foot in the door; it's all about connecting and being social.

Styling

Styling has been something that I have always done naturally. I've been styling my friends and family since forever. I did the same thing with styling that I did with modeling. My first paid gig was a styling a model name Whitney. She's from Florida and is now a close associate. We had an amazing few days shooting all kinds of looks. I used the pictures I got from styling her to start my portfolio, and from there I was getting lots of paid gigs as well as doing free gigs (only if they were creative and useful to my portfolio). I love styling, because it comes so naturally to me and it's something I will hold near and dear to my heart as I pursue my number one dream.

The point is, I was successful at the things I put my mind to, and although I didn't become famous—because that wasn't the goal and also because I didn't go as hard as I could've—I got the satisfaction I wanted. That is success to me. Everyone's definition of success is different. At this very moment, sis, I am stressing while writing this book and working on promotion, which requires a lot of time, and launching an affordable clothing line for girls like us. I always dreamt about these things happening, but I never in a million years thought it would come true. There are days when I get frustrated and depressed because it's only my mom and me operating things, and I don't have a job at the moment, which puts a strain on things as well. *But!* I will not give up. I know God will not lead me astray!

Turn your dreams into goals.

Goals

"Set your goals high, and don't stop until you get there." —Bo Jackson

Who do you want to be?
What are five short-term goals you have?
What are five long-term goals you have?
How are you going to get there?

I got my GED at seventeen years old and had always dreamed of working in retail. When I wasn't yet old enough to work, my mom talked to a guy she knew who owned a wholesale store in the garment district in NYC. I worked for him for $7.00 an hour off the books from about 10:00 to 7:00 with a 30-minute break. You couldn't tell me I wasn't a young woman, getting to the bag. I had my own job, I got my diploma, and I was on my way to starting college that September. I had turned my dreams into goals that were accomplished, and I was on an all-time high! My major goal then was to work at the Gap, so I interned at places for no pay just to add more to my résumé. About a year or two later, I got a job at the Gap on Fifth Avenue while attending Berkeley College.

As I matured, I realized that working for someone my whole life wasn't going to cut it. Although my ideas for my t-shirt line were flowing, I knew I had to think bigger. Because I love retail and styling, I knew that I had to work toward having my own store. So I worked and learned, learned and worked. I went on to work for Bebe as a stylist/visual merchandiser and at

J. Crew as sales support while interning at places and styling on the side. I got the chance to wear different hats, being in different roles in the industry, which prepared me to own my own store. I became a sponge, soaking everything up, oftentimes working for little to no money. Coming from the hood, where people expect you not to know anything and not to have any experience, I had a lot to prove. As I said in the Dreams chapter, I wanted to model, so I took the necessary steps to get there; I wanted act and style, and I took all of the necessary steps to do so. You must have goals in life. You must work hard to see those goals accomplished. You owe it to yourself to see how far you can go.

Say you want to do hair: while you're in high school, you should see if the owner at salon near you will allow you to sweep or wash hair for a few hours on the weekend. While you're there, your job is to learn as much as you can, pass her rollers, answer phones. Think like this: "Once I graduate high school, I am going to hair school, and when I finish hair school, I am going to work at a salon part-time and go to school for business or take business classes part-time and work at a salon full-time." The reason for the business classes is to learn the business aspects, so you can open your very own salon.

As long as you have a goal, a plan, and you are doing everything you can to accomplish your goal and execute your plan, you will never lose.

Example of a goal to become a singer:
1. Take singing lessons
2. Practice singing everywhere you go
3. Try out for talent shows

4. Find a studio
5. Get used to recording
6. Try out for singing competitions

And so on and so forth. You must have goals, whether they are small or big. Step by step, you must do what's needed to accomplish them.

Money

"The art of living easily as to money is to pitch your scale of living one degree below your means." —Sir Henry Taylor

Although I've been making my own money since I was about twelve or thirteen from babysitting and braiding hair, I was never taught to save money. Had I known then what I know now, I would've been a millionaire by now. Saving is something I will instill in my kids. I learned to save on my own. I do regret not saving all of the times I could have though. Last year I made a promise to myself and God that if he blesses me with a job, I will do what's right by managing and saving, and that's exactly what I have been doing every chance I get. Money allows you the freedom to go where you want, when you want. Having financial freedom is one of the best feelings in the world. When my mom was out of work for a while, I was working and getting paid good money. There was no better feeling than being able to pay my mom's bills and my bills, and buy whatever she or I wanted.

When you have money of your own that you worked hard for, you're less likely to put up with a guy who has money and is treating you badly. A lot of females put up with the guy they're dealing with because he buys her nice things. What I am advising you to do, little sis, is to save every chance you get. Budget your money and don't waste it on nonsense. It's so important to know you have it if you need it—your *own* money in your *own* bank account There's nothing like a smart girl with stacks on deck! Be about your dollars!

Fighting, chasing a dude, running around ratchet, and he-say, she-say: all of that should be the least of your concerns because your main focus is to remain focused on your money! The sooner you learn that, the better off you'll be in the long run when you hit your twenties. Your bank account will be stacked and your credit will be right! Good credit means everything in this world, just like your reputation. Protect them both with your life.

Because I am following my dreams of becoming a successful author and entrepreneur, I do not have money coming in like I did before, but it's okay because every dollar I get, I spend wisely and I am learning even more how to be smarter financially. So when I do start getting more money, I'll be wise with how I spend it.

Check	$200.00
Pay to Self	$50.00
Carfare	$30.00
Cell phone, hair, etc.	$120.00

This chart is an example of how you want to budget your money if you get paid $200 a week. At the end of the month, you should have $200 saved from saving $50 per check. At the end of the year, you'll have $2,400 saved up. That's better than spending all of your money on nothing and not having anything saved.

Post-Script: I ended up getting an amazing job (that I am no longer at). I took my money, saved more than I have ever saved before and paid off all of my personal debt. Now I am working in a dream position while I pay off student loans.

Fast Money

Dudes aren't the only ones chasing that quick dollar. I know plenty of females who steal and resell what they steal, sell drugs or their body, are down with scams, or pimp and strip for the love of that quick dollar. Baby, listen: selling your soul for something that will never bring you true happiness isn't worth degrading yourself and putting your freedom at risk. Not only that, sis, but also your self-worth is too important. There is absolutely nothing wrong with that 9-to-5 McDonald's job, retail gig, or sweeping hair in a salon for low pay until you can get where you want to be. As long as what you are doing is legit and respectful to yourself, God will make sure you shine bright. There is nothing like working hard and smart for your money then going to cash that check.

When you work hard for your money, you learn to treat it way better than your parents' money. Imagine you had sex for a few dollars to buy some shoes, then something happens where you get robbed or they get dirty or lost. You're going to be mad, but more importantly, you're going to be hurt because you sold your soul to get them. You could be the type who doesn't care and just goes and does it again to replace them, but if the thought "Damn, I just sucked, fucked, stole, or scammed for that" crossed your mind, then you have somewhat of a soul left. In that case, come to grips with yourself and stop it, get a decent job, and work hard for what you want.

Don't get me wrong—I know respectable women who stripped because they were at their wits' end and needed quick money, so they stripped to get what they needed while not allowing themselves to get caught up. However, nine out of ten of females go in with a plan and never come out with it. My point here is that if you stay on the right path from now on, being young with your whole life ahead of you, god willing, you won't need to do certain things to get money. I don't judge because there are many amazing women out there that enjoy what they do and see nothing wrong with it. But as a young woman, you have so much more to look forward to and so much time to get it done.

Materialism

"Keep your life free from love of money, and be content with what you have."
—Hebrews 13:5

There is nothing wrong with being a material girl. What girl on this earth doesn't love bags, shoes, clothes, and jewelry? When it becomes an issue is when you talk down to those who don't have all that you have. What turns me off about a lot of females who are materialistic is the fact that they feel it's only about name brands and that those who don't have them aren't doing it right. Or when name brands and trends are all they talk about. I give props to those who have it and are doing it, but I feel it's classier to "just do it" (as Nike puts it). There's no need to be stuck up, cocky, and rude about being a material girl. That just makes you look like you're not used to having a lot. Just because the next female doesn't have it or do it like you, doesn't make her any less of a material girl than you.

I mean when you have "it" and you're doing "it," "it" speaks for itself. That is what being a material girl with class is all about. Having natural bundle hair is a trend, and all the time I see females calling other females *basic* because they wear pack hair. To me, that shows how weak-minded that female is, because if she thinks having a certain type of hair makes you official she has a lot to learn. A guy will play a cocky material girl who wears Christian Louboutin red bottoms and Celine bags for a girl wearing Bakers shoes and $10 jeans as long as it looks right.

The Joneses

Trying to keep up with the Joneses is one of the worst things you can do. When you spend money just for show to try and match others, you are ignoring all of your potential. Also, most of the time you end up broke, busted, and disgusted. The Joneses either have the money to spend and actually love nice things, or they are putting on a front by trying to keep up with the Smiths. All in all, *just be you!* As far as trying to keep up with other people, I've never really done that. My mother always had me doing what others weren't, so keeping up wasn't on my agenda. There are dudes and girls trying to floss in cars they can't afford while living at home, spending money on clothes that cost as much as their rent, and spending money in clubs every other night when their bank account doesn't match with their lifestyle. All to keep up! You have everyone in the hood wearing hood-uniformed fashions. The dudes are in Gucci, Pelle Pelle, and Monclers, and females are in Ugg and have Speedy Louis Vuitton bags. Everyone looks like clones. Juicy

Couture jewelry sets, VS sweat suits—one word for these girls is *uniformed*!

Spending to keep up with the Joneses: it usually happens because someone has no style of their own. And there are the ones getting pregnant and wanting $1,000 strollers when they don't even have that in the bank, when they've never even saved $100 before, when they don't even have a car. All because they want to keep up or be better than the next. It kills me how people will live beyond their means just to keep up. It's one thing if you have it to spend and like nice things, but it's another if you don't and just want to fit in.

It's all about *doing you* and *being you*!

Independence

"The art of independence is not giving anyone the power to take anything away from you, whether it be materialistic or emotional."
—Unknown

For as long as I can remember, I have never been the type of girl to depend on a guy for anything. It was natural for me to be independent, being raised by a single parent. But once I got into a relationship where the sex was great, the money was good enough for me, and the sweet nothings were like music, I became dependent on it *all*. When I needed extra money and I was mad at him, I'd make things better between us just because I knew that I'd get some money from him. I wasn't using him; I just became dependent on him. I remember him telling me, "If you come with me for the weekend, I'll pay for you to get your hair done." At that time I was jobless and wanting a new 'do, so I went. I wanted to be around him to get all of the things I depended on and then some.

Sis, when you know better, you do better. Now that I know my worth, when I look back, I'm like, "Wtf was I thinking?!" But the thing that I want to emphasize is the importance of having your own money so you won't have to settle to get what you want. Love yourself so that you do not become dependent on some one else's love for you. Tell yourself sweet nothings so you don't have to rely on him to tell you. Work hard for your money so you won't have to be financially dependent.

Don't depend on anyone or anything but *God*. Those who depend on drugs and alcohol to feel better about a situation, when the high and drunk is over, the pain is still there. When you depend on your friends to go places because you don't want to be alone while out, you end up stuck in the house if they don't want to go. When I got old enough to go out to lounges alone, I did; I go to clubs and events alone. I get told all the time that I am *bold*, especially when I went to Miami for a weekend by myself. Doing something like that shows how independent you are and how much of a real go-getter you are. Usually when people think of independence, they automatically think of financial independence or independence from the opposite sex, but it's not only about that.

#MeToo

Molestation

"Being able to be open allowed me to feel even more free because it no longer felt like I was hiding something." —Epiphany Kendell

This is a serious subject that happens all over and in all kinds of households, no matter where you're from. And if it happened or is happening to you, you should speak up about it. Do not be afraid! Just like rape, being touched by someone older than you when you are a child is a crime. When I was about seven or eight, I was touched by a female who lived across the hall from me. I always wondered why, at a young age, seeing a naked woman or man on TV intrigued me. It's crazy how I remember that and all of the negative things that happened to me at a young age more than the good things. Now that I am older, I know it is not safe to let your child be left alone with certain people.

Girls who have been touched have a high risk of growing up to be promiscuous, sleeping around, becoming quiet and nervous, having psychological problems, or liking to be handled aggressively. Those who have been touched can also grow to touch others as well, and it's not their fault; it's just what they know and what they've been through. From reading and watching shows like Oprah, I learned about this issue, and I know many females, some friends, who have been in situations where brothers, fathers, uncles, their mother's boyfriends, or other people in their lives touched them. It's far too common!

The effects vary. Some people aren't greatly affected, yet it is something that definitely should be talked about. If you have a child, you can't trust new boyfriends to watch him or her, not even if you're just going to the store. I believe it's healthy to speak to someone about it. I waited to tell my mom until I was in my twenties, and I know it hurt her a lot, but I am happy I talked to her about it. Being able to be open allowed me to feel even more free because it no longer felt like I was hiding something. It also helped our dialog and communication grow stronger.

Rape

"By not coming forward about rape, you make yourself a victim forever."
—Kelly McGills

Rape is serious: it leaves physical, emotional, and psychological scarring. A female getting the most sacred part of her taken away is *never* her fault! I have been in a situation where my "no" didn't mean anything and I wondered if putting myself in the situation caused it to happen to me. As females, we have to make sure we aren't putting ourselves in certain situations where that can happen—although situations like that shouldn't happen in the first place. Men who rape women or girls are sick! We females can't lead a man on, however. We must be very clear that sex isn't an option and never be alone in a house or room with a guy if you don't want to have sex.

See, where I messed up was telling a guy I wouldn't have sex with him but letting him go down on me. Guys think everything is a game, and every girl is playing hard to get, so you have to say what you mean, mean what you say, and let your actions speak even louder. You must not let him give you oral sex if you know you don't want to have sex with him. And make sure you aren't getting crazy drunk or high around a guy if you know you don't want to have sex. If you have been raped, talk to someone immediately. Holding it in is mentally unhealthy. I know a lot of people who say that females shouldn't dress too sexy and revealing, which I totally agree with—prostitutes dress half naked outside. *But* at the same time, no matter how a female dresses:

NO MEANS NO!

I think of it like driving: you have to think for yourself and these sense less guys out there. Showing too much skin attracts strays. At times they don't know their own strength, and some of them will go too far because they're hype excited and disgusting.

Parents

"We never know the love of a parent until we become parents ourselves."
—Henry Ward Beecher

Our parents help define who we are. Their actions and what they teach and show us determines who we are as we get older. My mother raised me, as I have said in previous chapters. My dad was incarcerated up until I was sixteen years old. If you are blessed enough to have both parents who are in a healthy relationship, cherish that.

Fathers

My dad and I have our ups and downs, and although he hasn't been there for me how he should've been, I've grown and learned to forgive and keep it moving. Even today, I feel like my dad doesn't do what he's supposed to do. Yes, he texts me telling me he loves me every day, but he never asks to hang out. To me, he's like some guys I date—they say one thing, but their actions show something different. He doesn't really know who I am or what I need because he doesn't ask. He waits until I tell him and still doesn't execute, which to me isn't what you're supposed to do as a parent, especially when you're a father who doesn't live with their child. It bothers me every now and then because I think to myself, "I could've been a lot closer to where I want to be if he played his part," but then I brush it off and keep it moving. I just see what I do not want in a man and pray I find better for my child.

Life is way too short to hold grudges against things we cannot change. Don't get me wrong. My father has good advice about certain things. I learned to be a chess player in life from some of the jewels he dropped on me, but time and attention matters just as much. Sometimes I ask myself, "If he was here in my life, would I have saved myself for marriage? Would I have dated nice guys? Would I have known how to love myself more?" Although my dad was around, I still had my mom's ex-boyfriend, who I called my stepdad. He taught me a lot and gave me lots of insight; I will forever respect him as a man and cherish what he gave me. Knowledge, street smarts, and—like my mom—the drive to want more from life. I have uncles who support me and push for me to be better than the average chick from around the way. I just wish I would've reached out more at a younger age; I might have avoided at least half the stuff I got myself into. But, hey, you live and you learn!

Mothers

My mother and I have always been close, but there was a time when I was so angry inside and angry with her for making mistakes that I didn't think mothers should. I was clearly young and dumb! I was disrespectful for a short period of time. I remember being out with my friends, and my mom would call and text asking what I was doing, and I'd get an attitude and say mean things to her. When an old friend of mine told me that she wished her mom would call and check in on her, I realized I had something special. My mom didn't always know how to communicate, and as I got older, I respect-fully started to show her where she went wrong, and from then on things got better. We learned how to respect each other and each other's space.

I used to see other mothers going out and dating and wonder why mom wasn't doing that. I asked her, and she said, "I already did that. That isn't where I am in life." What I am so blessed for is the fact that I would come in drunk from being out with friends and my mom would be up waiting to hear about my night. That is so special to me. There are mothers out there who still act and dress young, trying to get their youth back after missing out from having kids. There are mothers out there still having kids with their kids. And I'm not here to judge, but I really appreciate my mom so much more today than I did when I was younger. Growing up, my mother never really sat me down to speak to me about sex or guys until I got into it on my own, and I would've loved for her to have spoken to me about it before. But it is what it is. Once I started getting into situations, my mother would tell me her personal stories and how she overcame them. But I still did what I wanted to do, which definitely wasn't the right move.

And what I am telling you, sis, is to respect your mother and father. Our parents lived their own lives before we came along. If I could go back and fix one thing, I would have listened more to those who came before me. If your mother or father is telling you a certain individual isn't for you, whether it's a friend or a guy, do yourself a favor and *listen*; take the advice that's being given. You will save yourself a lot of trouble and heartache. Respect and appreciate when your mom or dad calls to see if you're okay and wants to know where you are. There is a young girl somewhere wishing they could have the love and affection of someone who cares. And if you are that girl wishing you had someone, I say reach out to a close family member like an aunt or older cousin that has a good heart, or even a neighbor. Sometimes those who aren't family treat us better than someone we share the same blood with.

Family

"Blood doesn't necessarily make one family." —Epiphany Kendell

Family is important, but as you grow you will see that blood doesn't necessarily make one family. Someone you call a friend might be more loyal and respectful to you than someone you're related to. I grew up closer with my mom's side of the family, and with one of my cousins on my dad's side. She and I were close growing up and we lift each other up. They say your cousins are your first friends; mine were more like my sisters. We argued and said mean things to one another growing up, but as we've gotten older, we know how to have grown-woman discussions without attitudes. I see sisters and cousins fight all the time, but I feel like arguments should never happen where outsiders can see. It isn't anyone's business, and one of you should be big enough to walk away from a situation that might occur outside. I must say, the friends I have been blessed to meet and call my sisters have been amazing. Loyalty and trustworthiness makes friends family, in my eyes.

Keep an eye out for those family members who hate, because envy is a mother, and those close to you can hurt you the most. But on a brighter side, cherish the moments you have with your family and take heed to what they say. You don't want to be like me and miss all the jewels or good advice that family drops. And learn to have discernment when it comes to who to take advice from and who to not. Usually when a wise person is giving you advice they will tell you why they are able to give you the advice. For example, this whole book is me telling you why I am able to tell you what to and what not to do. But I also understand that you still have to learn on your own. A hater will advise you on things they know nothing about, they will also lead you on the path of self-destruction.

Friends

"One loyal friend is worth ten thousand relatives." —Euripides

This subject is essential to young females all over. Whether you're in the hood or not, friends help mold and shape who you are as a young woman. Growing up, we either have the same friends or we make new ones. At times we don't want to go out and make new friends because we are so used to the ones from around our way. That shouldn't be the case; having friends from other neighborhoods will help you learn and will expose you to new things. I have never had a problem making new friends, because my mother taught me to be outgoing, and because we moved back and forth between upstate and NYC, I had no choice but to get used to meeting new people.

Real friends are happy for one another no matter what one is going through in life. If you are having personal issues and cannot be happy for your friend, let her know, "Listen, girl. I am happy for you, but it's hard to show it right now because of my situation. I'm going to take some time to get my head right so I can be there for you and be my joyful self." Friendships are another kind of relationship, and it's all about *communication*! I have had a crew of four friends for a short period of time in my life, but before then and as I started growing, there were only two of us. When there is a group of you, there is high chance of there being secrets being told behind each other's back or jealousy that isn't healthy. So be careful with situations like that. When there happens to be an issue between two of you in a group, it's best to discuss it among one another. If you are a third party listening to both sides, you shouldn't judge or take sides. It would be okay to mediate; having someone mature there to mediate is the best move.

Some of us take friendship seriously and some of us don't. Some of us look at being loyal a certain way, and some of us don't know what it's about at all. Real friends tell one another how they feel about something that another said or did. She doesn't go tell everyone else before her friend, because she knows that will stir up drama. And if she is your friend, you don't want to bring middlemen into the situation. When there are three or more of you and arguments happen, be very careful, because the middleman doesn't always want what's best—trust when I tell you. There is going to always be someone left out because friends usually start in twos and grow into more. So when the two who have been friends for a long time get into a fallout, that will be the third wheel's opportunity to add fuel to the fire (if she's that type). It happens all of the time in many situations, so be aware of that, because it can make things worse between you and your closest friend. A healthy jealousy is normal within friendships, but it shouldn't last longer than two minutes. If your friend has something you wanted or like, it's okay to be jealous for two minutes, then it should pure happiness. Personally, I think it should be that from jump, but we are all human and you can't tell anyone how to feel. If someone gets jealous, that's because there are things within her or in her personal life that she isn't happy with, so that might be the only way she can feel at that time.

Within a group of friends, there are always different personalities—loud, quiet, fast (promiscuous, sexually active), virginal, etc., which is great, because you can learn from one another. But the most important thing is that you girls stick together. Do not let money or guys come in between you. If you like the same guy, *no one can have him*! If one of your friend's boyfriends tried to talk to you, you need to pull her to the side—*do not tell anyone else in the group*—let her know what happened and say, "I know you like him, but I had to let you know and I didn't tell anyone else." That gives your friend the chance to choose to stay with him or cut him off without everyone else's judgment or opinions. Friends do not tell each other's secrets while they're still friends or after they aren't friends. Friends do not sleep with or date each other's boyfriend while or after they aren't friends.

Friends do not judge each other. We all go through difficult situations, and just because this isn't your season to go through something doesn't mean it's not coming. Friends do not compete in a negative way with each other. An example of friendly competition is if your friend gets an A on her test and you get a B. You can say "Oh, I'm definitely getting an A next time." Friends are sisters without the same blood that God brings to us. I have been in many situations where I didn't properly know how to communicate with friends, and vice versa. As I have grown, I've surrounded myself with females who know how to communicate. I learned where I went wrong in the past. I've experienced situations where someone I considered a friend wasn't happy in her life, so whenever I had great things going on in my life, she didn't want to hear it. She would cause an argument and throw everything she knew about me that was negative in my face. Of course I have forgiven, but now I know that I can't trust everyone.

As you grow, you'll fall and make mistakes and you'll learn how to handle certain people and situations. I've also experienced when someone I considered a friend said disgusting things about me after we were no longer friends. Again, it got to the point when I realized I can't trust people. There will be females who have underlying feelings, meaning they front like they're your friends, but underneath it all they really despise you and everything you do. They pretend to be what you're about, just to have whatever perks there are when hanging with you. You won't truly know if a person is for you until you have a fallout and see what's real! You see a person better by not looking at them.

One last thing I want you to know is that as you get older you will know (if you don't already) that certain friends or associates are for certain things. You'll see you have friends you can be ratchet in the club with, friends for classier events, those you can tell secrets to, and those you can't.

The 10 Friend Commandments

1. No sex'n the exes.
2. Tell the truth even it hurts.
3. There's nothing wrong with a little friendly competition, but don't compete with your friends. The object is to win together.

4. No holding in feelings. Express yourself! Bottling up leads to hate.
5. NEVER tell your friends business/secrets when you're mad or no longer friends.
6. Always support your friends' goals and dreams, even if you don't agree.
7. Remain LOYAL, even if you're not speaking at that moment. Another person should never feel comfortable talking about YOUR friend to you.
8. If your friend is slipping, catch her and bring her back!
9. If she got it, you got it. If you got it, she go it. But don't take advantage.
10. If you see something, say something. Even if she gets mad, at least you did your part.

Gossiping

"Gossip is the devil's radio." —George Harrison

The whole female gender gossips. Males do it too, just in their own way, which is one of the many things that separate males from females. But negative, vindictive gossiping can cause a lot of heartache and sadness. The thing about gossiping is that it should only be done among close friends; it shouldn't be a he-said, she-said kind of thing. It's okay to say to your friend, "Girl, did you see what so-and-so had on? She looked crazy!" or "Did you hear what happened?" Although we shouldn't be judging anyone, we're human. That's what we do. But when it's someone you don't even rock with like that telling you "I heard so-and-so say that she didn't like you," and so on, that's a no no. It will cause all kinds of chaos. When someone who's not in your circle comes to you wanting to gossip about someone else's situation, *shut him or her down!*

Let them know you don't have time for that. Let them know you are focused on your goals and dreams. Let them know that everyone goes through something and that maybe they should go and ask the person if it's true and if they need a friend. It's always better and classier to be the bigger person. Have you ever felt like the world is yours and everything is going so well, then *boom*, someone comes to you with some gossip about you? And you're like, wtf? It's happened to me far too often! One thing I learned from my father and my mother about situations like that is to *watch the messenger!*

Trust

"Love all, trust a few, and do wrong to none." —William Shakespeare

Trust is something that people should work for, but on certain levels and in certain situations you should trust a person until they give you a reason not to. I have trusted many guys and girls after they have done things to hurt me, and I'm the type of person who's too forgiving at times. I can't play a grey area. It's either black or white; I like and trust you or I don't. I had to learn about trust on many different levels, business and personal, the hard way. Watch a person's actions more than listening to what they say, and don't always speak on what you know or what you see that they're doing.

Don't always show your hand. Trust people to a certain extent and watch how people act with you and others before you trust a person 100%. While doing that, remember that people make mistakes, and it's about what they do after the mistakes that determine whether they should be trusted again. Someone who gives an apology with actions showing that they were really sorry deserves to be trusted again. I've lied, cheated, said and done mean things; I learned my lessons and try hard not to do them again.

Friends and Trust

It's unfortunate that the only way to really know you can trust someone is when you or your friend's loyalty is put to the test. It's important that you figure out what trust means to you, so you can reciprocate it to your friends. I have a new set of sister friends, and I was able to say what I need from a friendship and they were able to tell me what they need, because we've all been in past friendships that didn't work. I built a strong bond with one of my sister friends I grew up with. We haven't spoken in years because we went our separate ways, then we came back together better than before. That happened because I was so open with her about so much, which made her feel comfortable enough with me, then we were inseparable. I sort of learned from trial and error how to point out the real from the fake, as you will.

Guys and Trust

As you've learned from reading previous chapters, it is not okay to trust a guy sexually by not using condoms. You cannot trust being with a street dude, because it will always take a real situation to happen for you to see what kind of man he is. As far as trusting what a guy says, it's okay to believe him, but as I've said, *watch* what he does. If his actions do not match up with his words, then you have your answer.

Peer Pressure

"If you follow the crowd, you might get lost in it." —Unknown

I myself haven't experienced peer pressure. I thank God, because Lord knows what I would allow someone get me into, on top of what I already got myself into. *But!* I have seen others affected by it; I've seen girls start trouble with other girls because their so-called friends pressured them into it. Females lose their virginities because they were peer pressured by their so-called friends. And let me tell you, the girls that pressure you into having sex are either mad they lost their virginity, were raped and don't want you to have your virginity, or are virgins and pretending to have had sex. Then there are those who will pressure you into trying drugs because that's what they do, or because they're addicted to it. It only takes one time doing certain drugs and you could be gone for life. Have a mind of your own, and keep your eyes wide open for those who want to secretly bring you down.

How the World Sees You

Attitude

"Weakness of attitude becomes weakness of character." —Albert Einstein

Every girl from the projects is assumed to have a bad attitude that most of the time comes from the environment we grow up in. Living in the hood, everyone expects us to be tough and to fight for our reputation, when we can actually be tough and well-respected without physically fighting to get our point across. And, see, what happens is we get so accustomed to acting a certain way that when it's time to go into the working world or a world outside of the one we are used to living in, we carry that with us. *No bueno!* I learned the hard way about the repercussions of having a bad attitude. Because of my bad attitude, I quit jobs and burned bridges with people who could've helped me progress in life. I didn't like who I was: short-tempered and freaking out on people who deserved it and on those who didn't—all because I didn't realize what God had blessed me with. At that time, I was working and doing styling gigs. I didn't have man problems, so what the hell was I mad about?

A lot of us have a problem with authority and with people who have different personalities and different backgrounds, because we are used to what we are used to. What I am here to say is: leave your attitude at home. Do not bring it to school with you, do not bring it to after-school programs, do not bring it to your summer yummy (summer job) or to your regular job. If you cannot learn when to act accordingly, you will never prosper in life. Do not be known as the typical black *angry bird* from the hood! Yes, I know that sounds harsh, but that's exactly what you look like when you're twisting your neck, yelling, pointing your finger, and being this tough girl that you do not need to be.

Now I also know that most of us have a right to be angry because situations at home are unbearable to deal with, so it's easy to come outside into the world and take it out on any and everyone, even ourselves. If ever you have anyone around that has positive vibes, who's more mature than you, someone who can offer you sound advice, go to them. Talking it out has always helped me.

Stay as positive as you can and around as many positive people as you can. You have to say to yourself, "Okay, I live in these projects. I can either become a product of my environment by dropping out of high school, becoming washed up, getting pregnant, gaining a bad reputation for sleeping around, having no job or self-respect, *or* I can finish high school, go to college (if that's what will move me toward my career), get a job, focus on my goals, and work on becoming the me God created me to be.

It's all about your attitude!

Bitterness

"Growth in wisdom may be exactly measured by decrease in bitterness."
—Friedrich Nietzsche

I feel that bitterness is something you have to be taught at a young age, because it seems to pass from generation to generation for many women. The mother was bitter about men or a man who did her wrong, so the daughter becomes bitter too. I see grown women looking tired, worn out, and walking with a frown all because a man hurt them. First and foremost, as your big sister who truly cares about you, I am telling you now: you will experience heartache and disappointment caused by a guy. It's inevitable, and the best of us get through it with tears behind closed doors and a smile in public. *Never let them see you sweat.* Never allow the mistakes of a guy affect your life in a negative way to the point where you feel all guys are the same, or that because he did you that way, the world is against you. I know plenty of females who go through difficult things with their man, and when he upsets her, she takes it out on everyone else; there are even those who take it out on their kids.

I have plenty of so-called reasons to be bitter, but I wouldn't dare act with bitterness. I believe that if God brings you into a situation, he'll bring you through it, so why bother being bitter? Bitterness causes stress. People won't want to be around you, which will cause depression and wrinkles because you're always frowning. *Who wants to have no friends or family to be around? Who wants to age early?* Just because your mother is mad does not mean you have to follow in her footsteps. Just because your mother got treated a certain type of way does not mean that will happen to you. A guy will do what he wants to do, but the level of respect he has for you depends on what you allow him to do and what you allow him to get away with.

Fighting

"The only thing you should be fighting for is your way out the hood."
—Epiphany Kendell

This is something that gets me sick! I wasn't raised to be out there fighting. My grandmother and mother taught my cousins and me to be ladies and to have class. I've been in two fights my whole life, and they both happened because the other person decided to take their self-hatred out on me. I have watched so many females around my way get into so much drama, and I thank God it wasn't me. I find it so classless and poor for females to be outside scratching each other's face up, pulling the Remy out, breaking their acrylics. Nowadays people are putting fights on YouTube just for views. Why would you want to be on the Internet for something so negative?

People don't realize that those things follow you. Hiring managers Google people now to find out whom they're hiring to represent their company. Although someone's past shouldn't affect their future, it does; that's just how life works sometimes. I dislike seeing young girls fighting, because to me there is nothing in the world a young girl should really be that mad about. I read an article in *Essence* magazine on Jill Scott where she said, "If you aren't fighting for your life or dignity, you should try to handle the matter in a mature way." The fact that we are out here bullying one another—like, really? If we all live in the same neighborhood and we know the same people, no one is better than the next. If someone is talking smack, let them talk. As long as your space isn't being violated, you should just walk away. Don't listen to those who call you a punk or scary; they just want to be entertained. Don't be someone else's entertainment unless you're Beyoncé and get paid big bucks for it. And if you have anger issues and want to fight and be seen, get into boxing or UFC.

Rumors

"Never make negative comments or spread rumors about anyone. It depreciates their reputation and yours." —Brian Koslow

Rumors make me laugh! Ever since I moved back to NYC from Syracuse, there is always something being said about me. I'd go out on dates and have the guy pick me up from my house (which is something I rarely did unless I was sure about a guy), then rumors started that I was sleeping with guys for money. There was talk about how I was hopping in and out of cars, when half the time it was the same guy who happened to have more than one car. Then there was a rumor that I was sexing my close male friend. I've denied it so many times, and I used to get mad at him and curse him out for not denying it, but he's like, *"Yo, how many times you want me to say no? Fuck what they think?"* And he was right. It's so stupid because I've never ever denied dealing, dating, or sleeping with a guy. I've honestly never been ashamed of anything I've done or anything that has happened to me. People would be sick because I'd still walk around with my head high and kept the same attitude. The craziest gossip was that I was dealing with this guy from around my way who's rumored to have HIV. I was coming home from a styling gig. I got off the train and was flagging a cab down, I saw him and asked him if he was headed to the hood (which, mind you, I do that to anyone I see when I'm getting in a cab and they're waiting for the bus).

I got out of the cab near my building, which is a spot lot of people hang around. When I saw people, I knew they'd think something was going on, because that's how ignorant people are. The very next day, sis, I promise you my phone and text was off the hook and I was being approached by people saying "I know what I heard isn't true, but I wanted to make sure." A guy associate of mine said to me, *"Oh, I heard you mess with someone who has that thing."* I was so turned off. Like, how old are we? People love to believe rumors because it gives them something to talk about, and it gives them their very own soap opera.

Reputation

"A good reputation is more valuable than money." —Publilius Syrus

Your reputation, character, and respect are related. Once your record is dirty, even when you decide to change, people might say you changed, but in their minds they're going to remember you for how you carried yourself in public. The people in my neighborhood always said I acted "Hollywood" until some of them got to know me. Every now and then, someone says that I still think I'm "Hollywood," but I am secure with myself now enough to realize that if that's the worst they can say about me...fine by me. Little did they know, at the time they were saying that, I had low self-esteem issues. As far as sleeping around in my hood, I wasn't with it—I mean there weren't many guys I was interested in anyway. I dealt with two guys in my neighborhood, both known as "popular" and what some call "hood rich" because of how they dressed. All the girls loved them, and they loved all of the girls. And although I shitted where I ate twice, I've managed to keep my reputation intact 'til this day. People say, "Oh, she be out there having sex with all these dudes. Oh, she's out doing this and that." When I used to hear those kinds of things, I'd say, *"Prove it!"* It really doesn't matter what I was or wasn't doing—they could never, and still can't, truly say what I was doing because I moved how I moved—which was and always will be with *class*!

It's not worth it to have your reputation dragged through the dirt for popularity around the way. I see a lot of young girls sleeping around to get attention—some because they're lost and confused, some don't have the right guidance, some do it for money, and some because a guy who claims to like her told her that if she really likes him, she'll have sex with his friends. If any one of those applies to you, you should *stop now* while you're ahead. Take back your power! There are also girls who have a reputation for getting drunk outside, embarrassing herself, fighting all the time, and getting high with the neighborhood zombies (people who get high all day and walk back and forth to the store zoned out looking dead. No glow, no spark in their eyes). You don't want to be either of those girls, and if you already are one of them you should turn your life around *now*!

Do not allow people to have power over you to the point where if you make a mistake, you feel you can't change. That's what life is all about: *growth*. If your reputation is intact, keep it that way. People will try you: guys will test you to see if you'll give it up and females will try to get you to come out of your character. Do *not* let them! Listen, little sis, you have a *rep* to protect, so you better guard it with your life!

Image

"Image is everything." —Unknown

The way you look and carry yourself determines, in part, how far in life you will get. If you dress like a hood rat and act like a hood rat, that's exactly what you will attract in life. Who wants to hire someone who talks extra loud and ignorant, dresses hood with scarves on their head, pants that are too small, and a shirt looking like a baby tee? You're probably saying, "But Epiphany, who I am in the inside is what matters." Listen up, sis: people can't see what's inside until they get to know you, and if your packaging isn't together, they won't want to take the time to get to know you.

Image matters in more than just important places. It matters all the time, even when you are in the hood. Keep yourself together. Walking out side with dirty scarves, cold in your eye, plaque on your teeth, ashy feet, or stains on your clothes is straight up tacky! I also want to talk about hygiene and the face. I so hate to see a female whose face looks like it needs a facial. Listen, there are so many home remedies and cheap products you can use. Do not let blackheads and pimples build up on your face—take care of it. Keep your underarm hairs and pubic hairs shaved and fresh; I run into too many young women who smell and look like young men. You have to make sure you are a priority.

Your image is important because it's what the world sees. Those extralong, overly decorated, multi-colored shovel nails, long and thick showgirl eyelashes, that Wite-Out-looking eyeliner, and those black-lined lips all have to go, sis! Those lace fronts with the lace showing, those thirty-inch nappy weaves and wigs, the rainbow colors in your hair...Unless you're trying to get a job at the circus, I suggest you start all over.

Body

"Take care of your body. It's the only place you have to live." —Jim Rohn

Most of us aren't taught to take proper care of our bodies, in terms of eating properly and exercising. Those who live in better neighborhoods teach their kids early on to be active and eat right. A lot of us have babies, and women's bodies change after childbirth, but even for those who don't have any kids, we let our bodies go. There are actual MILFs out there who are over thirty and look better than teenage mothers. There is nothing wrong with eating Nana's cooking. We all love that good ol' soul food, but we don't have to look like it. Don't let yourself go, and if you did, pick yourself up!

I see some girls who look like they just gave up on themselves. Their hair is a mess 80% of the time and their teeth have rotted. One thing you definitely always want to maintain, sis, is your smile. Once your teeth are done, it makes you look so many years older. My mom is slim, so I take after her in height and stature. But I was always a bit thicker than her, which looked good on me. There was a time in my life when I was drinking, smoking, and stressing. And that is not a good mixture for someone young and attractive with no kids. I lost weight and was looking and feeling tired all of the time. An old friend of mine's grandmother told me to start coming over for dinner so she could fatten me up. That food, plus me being happy again, led me to get my weight back. And as I am writing this book, I am getting my weight back from losing it again, but this time was because of me being stressed out over a relationship.

I learned, and you should learn too, that your body is your temple and it's your job to take care of it! Eat foods that are healthy for you, work out, and stay away from toxic people, places, and things.

Hygiene

Hygiene is very important, especially being a female, and I've noticed that a lot of young girls aren't up on it. If you're deciding to have hair under your armpits, be sure to have the proper diet as well as being really on point with keeping yourself clean. That way, your chances of body odor are low. Not saying that a girl who decides to remove her hair shouldn't take the same precaution. It goes for your vagina as well: if you aren't into regular waxing, shaving, or hair remover, you should definitely do one of the three before your period comes. Because hair traps smells and sweat, so imagine the effects when you get your menstrual.

Social Media

"Social media should improve your life, not become your life."
—Ritu Ghatourey

There are times I do not want to log on and times when I just want to delete people off of my page, because of statuses like this on Facebook:

ALL YOU BITCHES ARE HATERS IM GONNA KEEP DOING ME BECAUSE I STAY GETTING MONEY AND STUNT'N

Mind you, the spelling is jacked up. But if you read that and think, "I can say and post whatever I want on my page," go ahead. Keep doing it; to each their own. There has to be some kind of filter though. What surprises me the most is that adults do not say anything about it. I went off about two times on Facebook and got checked by those who love me each time. Twitter, Instagram, and Facebook are becoming people's diaries and psychiatrists. Some things should be left for your personal life. I see females posting pictures of their child getting shots, pictures of their hospital delivery moments, pictures at gravestones. What really moves me is the fact that so many females get on social media cursing like sailors.

I'm like, damn, I guess they want to have their own reality TV show. To each their own, but my point is to have somewhat of a filter on your life.

Maybe it's just the way I was brought up, but I have far too much respect for myself, my mother, and the adults who know me to act in such a way. To see young women writing things like *"Diss [this] nigga got me going crazy"* and posting sexually explicit rap verses just makes me ask where the parents are. Listen, I understand we all do what we want to do, but proper parenting will have you thinking twice about certain moves you make. On top of that, it's the girls who can't spell who post the most ignorant statuses, who tweet the most ratchet tweets, and who post pictures that should never see the light of day. Posting pictures of your body parts, yourself in your panties, your tongue ring... it all speaks negatively to who you are. The only guys who are attracted to that are the ones just looking for sex or the ones who just don't care. You don't want to be that attention-craving female, because it won't do anything but get you fake love and no respect.

Another thing I want to tell you about is meeting up with guys you meet online; a few friends and I did that years ago when we were on Myspace. Of course, a bunch of us went with the friend who wanted to meet the person. But I can honestly say we were young and careless, and anything could have happened. I want you to know that it isn't safe. Females go missing all the time and those who are found are usually raped and bruised, mentally and physically, or dead. Those Lifetime movies about online dating, Facebook killers, and stalkers are real.

Respect and Self-Respect

"Self-respect permeates every aspect of your life." —Joe Clark

I've always been one to go hard for respect, in the sense that I don't allow a man to call me out of my name or play me in front of his friends or females. Self-respect is also about me respecting myself enough to deal with a guy who respects himself: who respects himself enough to use protection when having sex with multiple partners, to want to go to school or start a business, or to stay out of jail. If you deal with a guy who doesn't respect himself, that says a lot about your character and who you are. Because, as the old saying goes, "You are who you sleep with."

One thing that my mother always taught me was to have respect for myself and to put anyone who tried to disrespect me in their place immediately. My mom always carried herself with class, so I followed suit. And although relationship-wise I let disrespectful things slide growing up, for the most part in the streets people respected me. If a female didn't like me, the only way I'd know is by the way she looked when I walked by (which is nothing to me), and if a guy didn't like me because I didn't give him play, everyone else but me would know. I remember one time in high school this boy called me a bitch. Talk about shocked and appalled—I could not believe my ears He said he was going to have girls from around his way come and fight me So I made one call and my stepdad and ex-boyfriend came to the school.

I knew I couldn't beat a boy, but I wasn't worried about no girls. I just couldn't believe a guy spoke to me that way just to look good in front of people. He heard about my people coming up and never came around again After that, I saw him on 42nd street and he looked away quick! I could've ignored him calling me out of my name, but that would've allowed him to think he could do it again, so I had to nip it the bud.

As far as demanding respect in a relationship, any time I heard that my ex was up to something with females, I would walk away. Each time would be longer and longer. I was young, so of course I kept going back. After one last time, I finally really walked away. Every time I walked away, I got stronger and learned more about how to respect myself and have values. I felt as his girlfriend, I shouldn't hear anything about him and other girls.

I see grown and young women who curse like sailors in front of their elders, which makes me so sick! It's like, damn, you must really have no respect or expect anyone to respect your mother or grandmother. I get on the bus and hear females talking loud, cursing, and having inappropriate discussions about a bunch of nothing while the elderly is on the bus. So I am telling you, sis, if that's you, change your ways because that's ugly! No matter how pretty you may be, a female with no respect or self-respect is ugly.

In work settings, managers feel that because they are above you they can talk to you in any way, and I don't allow that either. I've had managers say slick things, and I not only called them out on it, but I brought them to their boss and got my point across right then and there. No matter where you are or whom you're with, do not allow anyone to disrespect you. At the same time, you must recognize the difference between someone teaching you a valuable lesson with tough love and someone flat out disrespecting you. Getting respect is important, but *giving* it is just as important.

Partying

"Work hard, party hard." —Every smart worker

We all love to party, and before we could get into clubs we were usually talking about it. I've been partying since before I was supposed to; that's why I slowed down and then stopped when I was at the age where I was able to club. Being into partying, being out, and having fun really put me in the mindset of wanting to live life to the fullest before I settle down. I was partying Monday through Saturday, and depending on the event, Sundays too! I loved getting dressed, styling my friends, going to a new spot with new faces, getting right, and *dancing*! I was never the type to go to the club to post up, look cute, sit and stand on couches all night. I didn't really dance too much with guys—maybe one or two depending on how I felt—but I did love to two-step and move to the music.

After a while, going out, knowing the bouncers, the promoters, and DJs wasn't fun for me anymore. I felt like I was doing it all for nothing. I knew what being in VIP with celebrities was like, I knew what not having to stand in lines outside was like, and then I started to ask myself, "How is this benefiting me?" Partying was fun, but I wanted to be connecting, getting money; I wanted to have a reason to be there. I stopped partying because I realized I was spending unnecessary money to party with club promoters who were getting paid, rappers in VIP who were getting paid to be there, and girls who probably have careers and can celebrate. After a while, it felt pointless to me.

Partying and the Fakes

As you get older and start to go out and about, you'll see that there are a lot of pretenders out there. A lot of guys pretend to be what they aren't, so don't go to the club looking for a man thinking that a guy popping a bottle and wearing all the latest fashions has it, because, sis, he could be fronting. There are females out there rocking the latest fashions, the best weaves, popping bottles, and in reality she's struggling. She's stripping, turning tricks, or spending her last to keep up. Don't get me wrong. There are definitely girls and guys out there who have it, but there are way more fakes, so just be careful about who you try to keep up with and why.

Party to celebrate life and your accomplishments; party when you have it to spend!

Drinking and Drugs

"It is easier to stay out than get out." —Mark Twain

I can say firsthand that smoking weed is not all it's cracked up to be. I started smoking real heavy at about sixteen years old, then I started looking at myself and realized I was losing weight and my skin wasn't as flawless and glowing as it once was. I was wasting money, and there were times I looked in my wallet and was like, "Where the hell is my money?!" Then I remembered, and said to myself, "Damn, Piff. You need to get it together." When I smoked weed, I got lazy, I was stagnant, and I just wasn't my vibrant self that I once was. I know so many potheads now who forget to do something or say, "Dang, I had to run errands, but I got high and got lazy." The thing is, weed essentially will enhance how you feel. It's also important to know which strain of weed it is you're smoking, but I won't go there. I will say from experience don't drink or smoke until you're mature enough and have all of your ducks lined up. In the words of Dame Dash "Don't smoke weed until you made your first million."

If all you're doing is chilling in the hood and smoking, the only things that will come out of that are bad memories from dwelling on what you want to do or are going to do, and a bunch of nothingness. Weed makes you lazy. It makes you not want to go to work or school, which then leads you to want to go chill with a dude. Then you'll find yourself hanging out with impaired judgment, and the "right" touch can have in you in a situation where your pants are off. Weed can be very dangerous, especially when it comes to going out and taking pulls of other people's blunts. Or going to hang out with a dude or a "home girl," and the weed is rolled up already.

Never, I repeat never trust anyone when it comes to drugs or drinking. I've seen and heard so many stories about females and dudes tripping off of what was supposed to be regular weed. Shit, I tripped off of purple haze when I first smoked it. I remember it like it was yesterday. But my point is, people pull pranks. They may actually smoke dust and don't want to say anything and will have you smoke it. You just never know. Better to be safe than sorry and leave the drugs for drug heads. And, sis, if you are a smoker, whether it's all the time or some of the time, people shouldn't know you smoke: you shouldn't be at BBQs blowing it down in front of people's parents, your lips shouldn't be black, and you shouldn't have pics posted of smoke coming out of your mouth. Everything you do should be done with class!

Drinking, as we all know, has an instant effect and will have us looking crazy! I was drinking at a young age as well, and boy oh boy, did I learn my lesson with that too! I remember my aunt letting my friend and I drink in the house, so one night we were taking crazy shots of Bacardi. She was telling us that we were doing too much, but we kept insisting that we were okay. All I remember is laying back, throwing up on myself, my aunt putting me in a cold shower, and me just throwing up everywhere. The only time after that when I got crazy drunk was for my twenty-second birthday, when I went out with a friend.

I see a lot of young women running around drunk (and saying they're drunk), which makes no sense at all. Everyone wants to promote being drunk off of that "hen dog" Henny, or loose off the Goose. If you want to do mature things, then be mature while doing it. Mature females with class know their limit, and although I think it's better to wait to drink until you're mature enough, those of you who aren't going to listen need to know how to have some class while drinking. Getting sloppy drunk, falling on the floor, throwing up everywhere, and letting dudes run trains on you is not what's up! I sip every now and then when I go out, and when I get home my grandma says "Pootah, don't forget to not drink so much; it's bad for your skin." She doesn't drink and neither does my mother, and they are two of the most beautiful women I know, so I definitely take heed.

Health

"To keep the body in good health is a duty . . . otherwise we shall not be able to keep our mind strong and clear." —Buddah

So many of us do not take our health seriously until something major happens. If you have Medicaid, use that thing like a black card. Go get all kinds of check-ups just because. Get your blood, heart, and brain checked out. If you aren't sexually active, make sure you're getting tested for HIV every six to eight months. If you are, get tested every three to six months. There are girls who never went to an OB/GYN appointment until they got pregnant, and there are those who never got an HIV test until they went to the hospital for something else. That surely isn't the way to go. You need to go to regular dentist appointments, and if you are experiencing pain you need to go get it checked out.

A lot of people ignore the pain by taking painkillers. Why would you numb the pain without going to see what's actually wrong? I know people who ignore what their body is saying to them, and things end up being worse than what they expected.

Your health is important, so make sure to nurture it. Nurture yourself! If you don't take care of you, how can anyone else?

Insecurity

"Don't let insecurity ruin the beauty you were born with." —Unknown

As a young girl, I was very insecure about a lot of things—one being my height. My mom is tall; I get my height from her. My mom is also slim with small breasts and no butt. But, of course, she's the most beautiful woman in my eyes. I take after her with my shape and height. In school, when other girls were hitting puberty, I wasn't. I didn't have boobs, my hips weren't spreading, and I wasn't gaining weight. So of course boys didn't want to flirt with me or pay me any attention. I was very insecure, but I didn't really show it too much—wasn't loud. I looked at every guy as a brother, and when a guy did show interest, I didn't take it seriously because of my insecurity. My mother always kept me dressed nice, so I paid attention to fashion. The thing about me though is that I was never the type to put people down because I was insecure.

I was never a follower either. I just looked at other girls and wished I had what they had. The funny thing is, most of the girls who bloomed fast were the ones who also moved fast, and those are the ones who got washed up fast! Don't let your body get you washed up because of the attention it gets you. Lots of girls use their bodies to get places. Don't be her.

As I've grown, I've become more secure with myself. It's weird, though, because when I am out and if people stare, I get a little insecure. Then I have to tell myself, "Piff, maybe they're staring because you look nice." I also get insecure about my creative work, but that's normal. What I want to tell you, sis, is that although someone may have what you think you want or something you *think* you need to make you "better," trust me, God made you exactly how and who you are for a reason. Love what you have and who you are.

You are one of a *kind*!

Jealousy

"The jealous are troublesome to others, but a torment to themselves."
—William Penn

Jealousy can be natural, but it should never last longer than a few seconds or else it turns into envy. There is absolutely no need to be envious of anyone or what they have. I remember being young and being jealous because some of my friends and most of the girls around me had big boobs, extra long hair, or boyfriends. Although I've felt jealous at times (over what I think is totally silly now), I've never wished bad things on a female because I didn't have what she had; I never threw shade because she had something I wish I had. As you get older, you learn to appreciate who you are and what you have. Your chances of being jealous will be slim to none because you become more confident in your skin. A healthy form of jealousy is if your girl comes in saying "Bam!" while showing off a promise ring. The first thought and feeling should be happiness, then it's natural if you feel a bit of jealousy. Like, "Omg chick I am so jealous. It's beautiful!" See! Happy, healthy, jealousy is okay to feel, but if it lingers, it's not healthy. And if you feel it from someone else, be aware; a green-with-envy person is dangerous!

There are those who may be envious of you and everything you're about. But a jealous female will do whatever she can to bring you down! There are females who will try to sleep with and get pregnant by your boyfriend because she's jealous of what you have, or she'll try to set him up with a friend of hers. There are jealous females who will try to cut your face up because you're attractive. For instance, those who played on my insecurities hated themselves and were jealous of what I had going on. Envy is disease, so watch the company you keep.

Haters

"Haters gonna hate." —Unknown

Will there be people who dislike you and everything you're about *just because*—just because they're unhappy with themselves, just because they don't understand how you can come from exactly where you're coming from but be upbeat and hold your head so high? Yes! That's how some people have felt about me my whole life, and I could not care less. Mind you, they don't even consider the fact that you could be going through worse situations than they are. Ever since I can remember, there have been females in my life who dislike me for *no* reasons. Females have actually admitted to having no reason for not liking me. I've never been the fighting type and never pretended to be, but for some reason girls always wanted to beef with me. I am an only child, so I never grew up fighting with siblings, like so many people do. Then there have been those who didn't like me for a reason, like the guy I was dating, or because the guy they're checking for is checking for me.

I really never understood how a female could dislike another over a guy. There are so many guys around that we can choose from. The funniest thing about this subject are the females who would be messing with my then-boyfriend would be so mad when I walked in the corner store or walked past them. I used to be like "Oh gosh, his ass is messing with way too many females out here." I've seen older women who are insecure, washed up, and have nothing better to do than to pick and hate on me. But see, sis, what's going on with women like that is they are mad that they no longer have their youth or the mentality to change their life.

Instead of making moves to live the life they dreamed of, they feel *stuck*, so they hate on go-getters like us! So pay the old heads no mind, either. You also have to watch out for those in your circle who secretly hate on you. They are the ones who have a real reason to hate because they actually know what you're about. They see your blessings pour in, they see your hustle. They actually know what you're capable of accomplishing and how much of a blessed and gifted person you are.

Hate is hate!

Bullies

"Bullying never has to do with you. It's the bully who's insecure."
—Shay Mitchell

Bullying happens far too often in today's age—in elementary school, middle school, high school, college, and among grown women (as seen on reality television). It's disgusting, and I can speak from experience. I was bullied physically and verbally for no reason at all. I was living in upstate New York. I was skinny, dressed nice, from out of town, had no friends and no sisters— perfect target for girls that have nothing better to do. Even living in New York City, I got bullied by girls who were big and unattractive. Girls who knew they could beat me wanted to fight, girls saying smart things, rolling their eyes, and sucking their teeth when I walked by. I just couldn't understand why people were acting like that toward me. Although I am not about that fighting life, at this time, I will not allow anyone to physically bully me.

Now when females walk by sucking teeth and doing all of those bird movements, I put my head up even higher and keep it moving. Before, I would have my head midway up but feeling heavy on the inside. I dislike seeing women bully other women, especially bullying a woman who isn't about that life. It's like, come on now, don't you want competition? If you are the one being bullied, talk to someone and find the courage to stick up for yourself. If you are the one that is bullying, I am here to tell you that deep down you hate yourself and you need to seek help, because only someone with a lack of self-love and self-esteem will bully.

Those who have started trouble with me back in the day are now congratulating me on my accomplishments, whether it's sincere or not. There are also those who are on the sidelines hating, but every successful person experiences that. I'm telling you, sis, the underdog *always* wins in the end. Never give up, don't down yourself, and never contemplate suicide. Your life is far more precious and God has too much in store for you for you to want to end it all.

Suicide

"Don't allow circumstances cause you to wreck your ship when god has plans on smooth sailing it through the seas." —Epiphany Kendell

I remember being in middle school and being bullied (by people who now follow me on social media). Everyday going to school or after school, I would try to stay out of the way so that I wouldn't somehow fall into a trap. There was this girl waiting outside of my classroom because she didn't like me and always had something smart to say when I walked by. One girl actually admitted to me when I got to high school that she's sorry and didn't like me for no reason. The people at the community center I attended were no better either. I got my hair pulled and clothes made fun of.

I remember crying in the mirror at home wondering why me, why I couldn't be pretty, why people didn't like, and so on. So I tried to choke myself to death. I knew nothing about suicide. I don't even think I was exposed to it (on television or in real life) at that time. I honestly do not know where the thought came from, but what I do know is I am so happy I didn't go further with it. Why? Because look at me now! God had all of these beautiful plans for me that I couldn't even imagine at that time, and it would've been all gone because I thought life wouldn't get better. I thought there wouldn't be a time where I wouldn't be picked on or getting my hair pulled or being threatened. I remember even after high school feeling depressed and telling my mother I needed help, so I saw a therapist for a little while. It helped to get the stress off of my mind and understand what I was feeling.

Life will have its ups and downs. Humans are cruel, I know. I know there are some of us who get the worse parent(s), or siblings, or the feeling that we've been put in the "wrong" neighborhood or even feel as if we're put in the wrong body. BUT what I know isn't wrong is having the chance to be alive! The higher power made NO mistakes.

Suicide doesn't only hurt you and your calling in life, but it hurts those close to you, even if it is that one friend. Suicide is the weak way out! It takes guts, strength, and a true Queen to be able to say "You know what? I refuse to allow my current circumstance to mess up my future!" Go seek help, go speak to someone, help yourself get to an healthy place by controlling your mind and emotions. Talk to yourself, tell yourself "Self, this is where I am right now, but it won't be where I stay."

Life doesn't get better. YOU get better! You are the captain of your ship, and God helps guide that ship. Don't allow circumstances cause you to wreck your ship when god has plans on smooth sailing it through the seas.

Underdogs

"Hate it or love it, the underdog's on top." —Curtis Jackson

In junior high, I got picked on for being flat-chested and not dressing like everyone else. I remember my jeans rising up when I sat down and I went home crying to my mom begging her to buy me longer jeans because I was getting picked on. My mom shopped at thrift shops for years, and a friend of mine told everyone, so I got picked on for that. In Syracuse, I wasn't guys' first pick. I only had one boyfriend in high school because only one guy showed interest. Girls didn't want to hang out with me, although I had three good friends who also had other friends. In the afterschool programs, everyone had their clique because they grew up together. I was from NYC and in my own world, and because I had my own style, some people felt threatened. After a while I started coming into my own, but the feeling of not being looked at or wanted around hurt like hell. If you, sis, are feeling left out, picked on, or lonely, just know that the *underdog* always rises!

Mistakes

"Forgive yourself for your faults and your mistakes and move on." —Les Brown

Oh gosh! Where do I begin on this subject? We *all* make mistakes—young and old, rich and poor, from the hood and from the 'burbs. Some mistakes we girls tend to make are fighting over dudes, having babies by the Stevie J of the hood, sleeping around, falling in love with the "flyy boys," trusting the wrong people, and following in our parents' footsteps. One thing about life that's certain is *change*! With that being said, only you can change you (with the will of God). So what if you slept around in the past, even if you just stopped yesterday, due to a lack of self-love? The fact is, when you decide you want to make a change, from that moment on... everything before is in the past.

Go for it! I still am learning to change my ways. I have to check myself about my attitude all the time; I have to check myself about being too nice or too mean to people. I've had to learn to get used to liking nice guys. It sounds easy, but it's not if you're not used to it. Do not allow people to tell you that you won't or cannot change. Do not allow anyone to tell you that you will always be some way or that it's too late.

For example, if you got pregnant at a young age, the naysayers might make you feel you cannot go on and accomplish things, and that is so wrong. The best thing about life and mistakes are that you gain experience from them. You learn and move on. Don't do today what you did yesterday; don't do what you did in your teens when you're in your twenties. Do not beat yourself up about your mistakes. Live and learn from your mistakes—I know I have.

Self-Esteem

"The worst loneliness is to not be comfortable with yourself." —Mark Twain

I suffered from self-esteem issues for a long time in secret. I never told anyone, not even my mom. Although there were people who called me pretty, inside I just didn't feel it. I used to look in the mirror and hate what I saw; I still can't believe I felt that way about myself. But I look back and say thank God for growth, self-love, and self-acceptance. I don't know where my low self-esteem came from or when it started, but I do remember getting older and being around people I considered friends, and it getting worse. They played a big part in how I felt about myself. They used to make fun of how big my head is, how big my lips are, and how slanted my eyes are, saying I look Chinese. I hated it! Once I was no longer around them, I started to love me even more! Everything they said was ugly is now what makes me stand out from every other girl.

Sis, whatever it is you hate about yourself right now and whatever people are making fun of you for are exactly what makes you different. That is the extra time God spent on you to make you special.

Love and Self-Love

"Our first and last love is self-love." —Christian Nestell Bovee

Love as we know is a beautiful thing. The first time we feel like we love a guy, we get all kinds of butterflies and our minds live in la-la land. The second time we love, we feel like love can't get any better, until the next time love comes again. Loving someone is beautiful, but loving yourself is even better. Self-love is something we have to be taught growing up, and at times, even if we are taught it, we can lose ourselves in relationships. The thing I learned about being in a relationship is that you must have your own life! *Must!* Your main focus should be school, working, or extracurricular activities. If you have too much time on your hands, it will have you thinking about him and calling him all of the time: Who is he with? What is he doing? Why isn't he with me? These are questions you do not want to ponder all day every day.

I am no life coach; I am only giving sisterly advice about what I know. **Self-love is the key to loving someone else and to receiving the love you deserve.** When I didn't love myself, I gave my body freely to those who were nice and to those who didn't deserve it. Not knowing how to love Epiphany, I allowed myself to be mean and ignore the guys who would've treated me like the queen I *now* know I am. When I didn't know how to love me, I allowed myself to help an ex sell drugs and I held guns and drugs in my bags and in my home, which was a violation to my mom and grandmother and our living situation, because if the cops wanted to come search my house it would've put them in a crazy situation. They are the only two who would've held me down and bailed me out had I gone to jail.

When you love you, it shows, which makes others want to love and respect you and come at you correct. Being able to go out and enjoy a movie by yourself is a step to loving and learning yourself. Not always needing a dude or friends to be with you is key to learning to enjoy your own company. I learned that from my mom. I used to wonder why she was never anxious to hang out with friends or a guy, and now I see why.

My Self-Love Contract

In the presence of God and my witness, I, _____, vow to love, honor, respect, cherish, and take time to get to know myself. I vow to forgive myself for the mistakes I have made in the past, as well as the mistakes I will make in the future. I vow to forgive those who have hurt me, for they know not what they do. I vow to always have faith and stay faithful to the God in me. I vow not to judge others, for I know not what they have or are going through. I vow to seek God first for any answers I may need.

I vow not to give my body freely to any man who is not my husband. I vow to get to know a man before I jump into any relations with him. I vow to eat right, drink plenty of water, and obtain a positive mentality. I vow not to bring the baggage from my past relations into my future one(s). I vow to pray and meditate daily for my mental and spiritual health. I vow to love open-heartedly and listen more than I speak.

I pledge to you, _____, my faithfulness and eternal love from this day forward.

_____
Signature

_____
Signature of Witness

_____
Date

_____
Date

You

"God resides within you and you must put god first." —Epiphany Kendell

At the end of the day, sis, I wrote this book for you. I wrote this book so you will understand that you aren't alone. We all go through experiences, some worse than others, but that's what life is about. Hard times show you that there is a God, and they teach you to work hard and have faith. I want you to know that until you are old enough and married, that it is all about *you*! Not a guy and not a baby. You must be stingy with your life. You have to do what makes you happy, what moves you toward a better, more accomplished, and successful life. It's all about your schooling, sports, working toward your career, having fun with your girlfriends. You must do all of the things you put your mind to while you are young and growing. People will say, "Wow, she really wrote this book. She really put her most insecure feelings and situations out there for people to judge her," or "Why would she put her business out there like that?" The answer is *you*! I did it for you, the young girl in the hood who needs someone she can relate to, to look up to. I wrote this so you can have inspiration.

Kimora Lee Simmons has been my inspiration, Oprah has been my inspiration, but I would have liked to been able to look up to someone around my age who came from a hood like mine. Oprah didn't have to talk about being raped, losing a baby, or her struggle with self-esteem, but she did to help encourage others. As you grow, you will realize that life is about helping as many people as possible without bringing yourself down.

I love me and I love the woman I am becoming. I have so many more books to write, but first I had to put this out there to clear the air, to really give you an idea of who I am, so that when you see my other works coming, you will know: Epiphany did all of this, she came from this, she experienced this—but she really did it. She did *everything* she said she would do. I am here to give you the blueprint. Life is going to be tough, but you can avoid a lot of unnecessary struggles if you play this game of life the right way.

Thank you so much for taking the time to get to know me. I pray you get inspired.

I love you,
Piff

Made in United States
North Haven, CT
23 March 2023

34441578R00057